MORTGAGE
YOUR WAY
TO WEALTH

MORTGAGE
YOUR WAY
TO WEALTH

The Principles of Supplemental
Real Estate Financing

Joseph L. Steinberg

Parker Publishing Company, Inc.   *West Nyack, N.Y.*

Dedication

This book is fondly dedicated to my parents,
Tillie and Louis Steinberg, with deep
appreciation for their inexhaustible supply
of warmth, affection, and confidence.

Introduction

This is the first published work dealing with second mortgage investments in detail. It offers you a unique insight into the philosophy and mechanics of a dynamic investment vehicle.

You need no knowledge of the subject — this book supplies all the information necessary to successfully participate in this potentially low risk – high yield investment field.

Second mortgages have traditionally been recognized as high yield investments. Their potentially conservative nature is not as widely understood. This book, through its Safety Formula and Ability-to-Pay Formula, will show how to build an investment portfolio more conservative than the mortgage portfolio of a neighborhood bank or loan association. Combining security with high income should be the goal of every intelligent investor.

The twenty chapters that follow contain all the information, forms, check lists, formulas, and advice needed for successful mortgage investment and management. They have been tested in the field. They work.

Included are the techniques of getting started, how you can begin your investment program with as little as $1500, organizing a group, finding mortgage investment opportunities, initial interviews, legal restrictions, closing the mortgages, managing your investments, building the portfolio, accelerating its growth, and liquidating the investments.

Special attention should be paid to more than two dozen forms; six charts, numerous check lists and worksheets; the laws of fifty states, the Virgin Islands, and Puerto Rico; the eighty sections and sub-sections of sample by-laws for an investment group; and the remarkable Safety Formula and Ability-to-Pay Formula.

INVESTORS will find an exciting new vehicle for unusually high income, extremely low risk, and minimum management needs.

ATTORNEYS will discover how to advise and service a rapidly expanding investment form. All the necessary material is included.

REALTORS will learn how to save sales, increase listings, and develop a new form of income.

ACCOUNTANTS, APPRAISERS, AND BANKERS will increase their skills as financial advisors by learning the fundamentals of supplemental real estate financing.

HOMEOWNERS eager to transform the passive equity they have developed in their property into useable cash will learn how to save thousands of dollars.

One clear caveat must be given and understood. The five extensive charts, presenting the laws of fifty-two jurisdictions for legal interest rates, maximum interest rates, corporate exemptions, need for written documents, and usury penalties should be viewed solely as general guides. Limitations of time, space, and skill preclude an analysis in depth of all the ramifications of the many diverse factors that affect the statutes. Changes by legislative amendment and judicial decree take place with astonishing speed and regularity. Consult the charts to gain a broad insight. See an attorney before you proceed.

Then, *Mortgage Your Way to Wealth*. And the best time to start is now.

Contents

Chapter   Page

Chapter   Page

Chapter   Page

Chapter   Page

Mortgage Your Way To Wealth

My Problem ... Buying and Investing ... Nothing Is Perfect ...
Unique Advantages ... Start with a Small Sum ... Seeking the
Proper Investment ... A Five-Year Plan ... The Portfolio in Five
Years ... The Cash Flow ... Not a Fairy Tale ... Higher
Earnings Available ... Lower Earnings Possible ... As an Individ-
ual or with a Group ... Advantages of an Investment Group ...
Investing as an Individual ... The Conservative Approach

My Problem

Singing the praises of second mortgage investments in order to
bring its importance to the attention of the reading public presents a
problem.

Remember the little restaurant you found, tucked away on a side
road? Its menu was superb, its dining room uncrowded. It was your
hide-away. But you, big mouth, told the world. Before long it became
everyone's hide-away. That back road soon seemed like a major
thoroughfare. You had to call ahead for reservations. The bar was
busy, the tables crowded. True, the food was as good as ever and the
atmosphere lost none of its charm, but it was no longer your
hide-away. It had become a public joy.

Will I do the same with this book about second mortgages? I know
that the benefits of mortgage investment are unique, that mortgages
are conservative and secure, that they require small initial invest-

ments. The return is high, the risk low. And at the moment, second mortgage investing is still a cozy little hide-away tucked away on a side road.

Now, mortgages are certainly not a deep secret. There are shrewdies all over this free enterprise society of ours who are energetically applying their skills to second mortgage investment. But they are a relatively small group.

Buying and Investing

There are a large number of people who buy mortgages. I am not referring to them. As I use the terms, buying and investing involve entirely divergent approaches. The buyer grabs. He accumulates. To him, a mortgage is a one-dimensional commodity, without variations. The buyer collects. The buyer gambles.

Not the investor. He studies. He evaluates. He chooses with care. And in the long run, the investor earns more than the buyer.

My problem is whether to make this private love affair a public romance.

A number of thoughts convince me that I have no choice.

1. An extensive presentation of the techniques of second mortgage investment would be a boon to those many thousands of people who are unaware that such an ideal investment vehicle exists.

2. By knowing the details of all the techniques of second mortgage investment, many people who might otherwise risk the penalties of collecting will be able to enjoy the benefits of investing.

3. An expanded understanding of the benefits of second mortgages, both to the borrower and the lender, will mean an expanded market.

Nothing Is Perfect

There are as many investment vehicles as there are investors' needs: Good investments and poor investments, conservative investments and speculative investments, secured investments and unprotected investments, transferable investments and nonnegotiable investments, liquid investments and nonconvertible investments.

And for each of them there are comparable investors: Intuitive and studied, cautious and bold, knowledgeable and neophyte, patient and restless, ambitious and conservative.

As a result, there is no form of investment that can properly claim to be perfect.

The wealthy man looks for a tax advantage, the restless man for an adventure, the knowledgeable man for a sophisticated challenge, and the ambitious man for wealth and power.

Most popular investments involve the use of sizable sums of money or the application of skills, experience, and knowledge meticulously and painfully gathered over the years.

The purchase of unimproved farmland at the outskirts of an exploding urban community will probably involve more money than the average man has available.

The creation and management of a portfolio of common stocks demands an understanding of the industries in that portfolio, continuing analyses of the individual corporations, and the experience which will enable the investor to apply those analyses.

Most popular investment forms involve a choice between a high return at a correspondingly high risk, or a conservative return at a minimal risk. In other words, the more you can earn, the more you can lose.

None of this applies to second mortgages. If it is true that no investment form is perfect, certainly mortgages come close.

Unique Advantages

Second mortgages have four major advantages which, in combination, are almost unique among readily available investments.

1. They are available to investors with modest capital.
2. They can return earnings far above average yields.
3. Capital can be invested conservatively, minimizing the risk of loss.
4. The skills necessary to enter the field with a command of all the basics are well within your grasp.

Start with a Small Sum

You can start with fifteen hundred dollars, a modest amount, and invest it at rates far above savings account or stock market yields. Yet your capital, while earning much more than your neighborhood bank or savings and loan association offers, can be invested just as conservatively as that same bank or association invests the funds entrusted to it, and in precisely the same investment vehicle—real estate mortgages.

There is at least one difference. A key difference. Savings banks and loan associations freely grant mortgages in an amount equal to 80 per cent of the value of the property, sometimes as high as 90 per cent. You would not. As a conservative second mortgage investor, you would average 70 per cent or less. That magic margin of security is your investment safety belt.

It means your money is safer than the bank's money—and earns much more.

Let's see how it works for a second mortgage investor.

Seeking the Proper Investment

Once upon a time there was an Average Joe. He had a small savings account, a decent job, and an adequate insurance plan.

He managed to save ten dollars a week, and had enough in his savings account to enable him to spare fifteen hundred dollars for an investment.

His problem was finding the proper investment. It had to be a secure one. He had no desire to lose his fifteen hundred dollars. Yet, being an Average Joe, he had the same thirst for a healthy investment return that captivates all of us.

A savings account of fifteen hundred dollars would earn sixty dollars a year sitting safely in the bank's vault, perhaps seventy-five dollars, but inflation would eat away at the value of the principal, and the return would be too modest. Inflation is said to cost approximately one and one-half per cent of the purchasing value of the dollar each year. Savings accounts earn approximately 4   per cent a year, sometimes   5. It is difficult to become enthused over an annual net return of 2 1/2 or 3 1/2 per cent.

The stock market is an attractive investment area, but Average Joe tried it once and was embarrassed by the results. He still holds one of the stocks. It fell so low his shares have never come within eight dollars of the price he paid for them four years ago. The stock market's dips, based upon real or fancied news, bother him. His cousin, forced to sell some stock to meet unexpected medical bills, was caught in a declining market and lost 16 per cent of his investment. Joe realizes that the market has great potential for gain, but he has neither the time nor the skills to become a student of the stock exchange.

Real estate is an exciting possibility, but owning investment property calls for skills, initial cash outlays, and experience he lacks. He has no confidence in his ability to become a successful landlord, dealing with tenants, negotiating with plumbers, or supervising a janitor.

A Five-Year Plan

Then he read this book. He learned that second mortgage investments earn a remarkably healthy return. And yet, by following my Safety Formula, he would have as conservative and secure an investment as any mortgage loan officer in his state. Better. More conservative. More secure.

He followed my step-by-step approach and set out on the road to becoming a private mortgage investor.

Choosing from among a number of applicants, he lent the homeowner of his choice $1,500 for three years at 12 per cent, the going second mortgage rate in his state. That mortgage loan paid $49.83 per month for 36 months.

Continuing to follow his regular savings program, he amassed $1,676.94 in the 18 months that followed by totalling his $49.83 monthly mortgage receipts and his $10 weekly savings.

On the eighteenth month he placed another $1,500 second mortgage, raising his monthly receipts from both mortgages to a total of $99.66. He continued putting aside $10 each week.

Ten months later, twenty-eight months after he started, he found he had accumulated another $1,426.60. Adding the $176.94 surplus from his earlier mortgage, he was able to place still another mortgage, raising his monthly receipts from the three mortgages to $149.49.

In eight months, thirty-six months after he started, he had a nest egg of $1,545.92 in mortgage receipts and weekly savings, plus the $103.54 surplus from the previous mortgage. He placed his fourth mortgage and held an uninvested cash surplus balance of $149.46.

But his receipts remained constant, for his original mortgage loan had been paid in full at the thirty-sixth month.

In the eight months that followed, he accumulated another $1,545.92, placed his fifth $1,500 mortgage, and added this surplus of $45.92 to his previous surplus of $149.46.

His receipts now rose to $199.32 a month. In the following six months, fifty months had passed since the investment program had begun. His regular weekly savings program, the monthly mortgage receipts, and his $195.38 surplus enabled him to place his sixth $1,500 mortgage.

His receipts now stood at $249.15 per month.

In the next five months, his receipts and savings reached $1,567.26, including the earlier surplus. Mortgage number seven was placed. At the fifty-fifth month, his monthly mortgage loan receipts were $249.15.

By the sixtieth month, he had a total of $1,623.01 in mortgage receipts, savings, and surplus. Thus, mortgage number eight was added to the portfolio.

Here is a graphic illustration of the mechanics of Average Joe's sixty months as a mortgage investor:

First month:

Mortgage #1 $1,500.00	$	49.83 Monthly receipts
cash returns		896.94 Eighteen monthly mortgage payments
		+ 780.00 Savings, at $10 a week
		$1,676.94

18th month:

Mortgage #2		
$1,676.94 cash	$	49.83 Mortgage #1
-1,500.00 mortgage		49.83 Mortgage #2
$ 176.94 surplus	$	99.66 Monthly receipts

$ 996.60 Ten payments
+   430.00 Savings
+   176.94 Surplus
$1,603.54

28th month:

Mortgage #3
$1,603.54 cash
-1,500.00 mortgage
$ 103.54 surplus

$ 49.83 Mortgage #1 ·
     49.83 Mortgage #2
     49.83 Mortgage #3
$ 149.49 Monthly receipts

$1,195.92 Eight payments
+   350.00 Savings
+   103.54 Surplus
$1,649.46

36th month:

Mortgage #4
$1,649.46 cash
-1,500.00 mortgage
$ 149.46 surplus

           Mortgage #1 paid off
$ 49.83 Mortgage #2
     49.83 Mortgage #3
     49.83 Mortgage #4
$ 149.49 Monthly receipts

$1,195.92 Eight Payments
+   350.00 Savings
+   149.46 Surplus
$1,695.38

44th month:

Mortgage #5
$1,695.38 cash
-1,500.00 mortgage
$ 195.38 surplus

$ 49.83 Mortgage #2
     49.83 Mortgage #3
     49.83 Mortgage #4
     49.83 Mortgage #5
$ 199.32 Monthly receipts

$1,195.96 Six payments
+   260.00 Savings
+   195.38 Surplus
$1,651.34

50th month:

Mortgage #6
$1,651.34 cash
-1,500.00 mortgage
$ 157.34 surplus

$ 49.83 Mortgage #2 paid off in 4 months
       49.83 Mortgage #3
       49.83 Mortgage #4
       49.83 Mortgage #5
       49.83 Mortgage #6
$ 249.15 Monthly receipts

$1,195.92 Five payments (less Mortgage #2 for
                                one month)
+   220.00 Savings
+   151.34 Surplus
$1,567.26

55th month:

Mortgage #7
$1,567.26 cash
-1,500.00 mortgage
$ 167.26 surplus

$ 49.83 Mortgage #3
       49.83 Mortgage #4
       49.83 Mortgage #5
       49.83 Mortgage #6
       49.83 Mortgage #7
$ 249.15 Monthly receipts

$1,245.75 Five payments
+   210.00 Savings
+   167.26 Surplus
$1,623.01

60th month:

Mortgage #8
$1,623.01 cash
-1,500.00 mortgage
$ 123.01 surplus

$ 49.83 Mortgage #3
       49.83 Mortgage #4
       49.83 Mortgage #5
       49.83 Mortgage #6
       49.83 Mortgage #7
       49.83 Mortgage #8
$ 298.98 Monthly receipts

The Portfolio in Five Years

Five years have passed. Let's see what Joe accomplished.

He invested $2,600 in weekly savings and $1,500 as an initial investment for a total of $4,100.

His portfolio at that moment included six mortgages, and would be itemized as follows:

Surplus	$ 123.01	
Mortgage #3	194.09	Balance
Mortgage #4	560.51	Balance
Mortgage #5	898.90	Balance
Mortgage #6	1,135.60	Balance
Mortgage #7	1,322.33	Balance
Mortgage #8	1,500.00	Balance
	$5,734.44	
	-4,100.00	Investment
	$1,634.44	Increase, or 39.9 per cent

The Cash Flow

These mortgages, however, would not be suddenly and magically paid in full at this five-year point. Oh, no. They would continue to earn interest throughout their lives. Their total remaining payments, including interest, would be as follows:

Surplus	$ 123.01	
Mortgage #3	199.32	
Mortgage #4	597.96	
Mortgage #5	996.60	
Mortgage #6	1,295.58	
Mortgage #7	1,544.73	
Mortgage #8	1,793.88	
	$6,551.08	Mortgage Receipts
	-4,100.00	Investment
	$2,451.08	Earnings, or 59.8 per cent

Not bad at all, is it?

Average Joe lived happily ever after. And immediately began his second five-year plan.

That is not a fairy tale. Thousands of investors throughout the United States are following this pattern. Many are growing much faster by starting farther up the ladder. If you have more than $1,500 in available surplus capital, or can save more than $10 a week, you can accelerate your growth. You can start with more than one mortgage—or with larger mortgages.

Higher Earnings Available

Actually, the return can be higher than I've shown.

The monthly receipts earn interest when banked between investments.

A surprising number of mortgagors pay off their loan a few months after the mortgage has been placed. In that case, the normal mortgage clause guaranteeing the mortgage 12 or more months' interest results in a windfall. This aspect is discussed in greater detail in Chapter 13.

The mortgage term used in this hypothetical case is three years. Experience shows that the average second mortgage is written for a period of almost five years. Earnings are considerably greater as the term increases. See Chapter 12.

When a portfolio has been created, banks will often loan funds on the strength of that portfolio in an amount equal to at least 50 per cent of the portfolio value. Using lower cost borrowed capital, and placing it at higher interest rates, creates a situation that sharply increases the return on the investor's capital. This leverage technique will be fully explored in Chapter 18.

Lower Earnings Possible

The return may be lower than I have outlined.

It may be necessary to purchase these loans from mortgage brokers. Commissions of 2 per cent of the mortgage amount are not uncommon. Thus Average Joe's eight $1,500 mortgages would have cost $240, a sum the remarkable earnings take well in stride. See Chapter 5 and 7 for techniques of minimizing this expense.

The rate of return for mortgage investments in your community may be less than the 12 per cent used in our illustration. The statutory limitations for each state in these United States is outlined in Chapter 11. Whatever the limitation, you will find that the vast majority of jurisdictions permit substantial earnings considerably higher than comparable investment returns.

You may find it difficult to time your investments well enough to keep your money working constantly. This problem, and its many solutions, are discussed in detail in Chapter 17.

Your mortgage may prove to be insufficient to protect your
ment. The value of the property may be less than the co
principals of the first and second mortgages. This will *not* happen ..
you follow the simple step-by-step details outlined in Chapters 8, 9,
and 10. I have evolved a system that results in a portfolio of mortgage
investments superior to that of the most conservative bank in your
community.

Investing as a Group

You need not approach this investment field only as an individual.
You can form a group, and depending upon its size, the individuals
could invest anywhere from $10 to $100, or more, a month. In
Chapters 6 and 7 I detail each and every step in the creation of an
investment group.

The creation of an investment group carries a number of advantages.

Because it comprises many members with their greater number of
contacts, it often results in more direct references and fewer broker's
commissions.

The members can be chosen for their backgrounds, gaining the
benefit of the skills of an attorney, an accountant, a realtor, a builder,
an appraiser, a credit manager, a banker, and the many other callings
that can be of value in this investment field. Further, many expenses
can be minimized or completely eliminated by utilizing the skills of
members of the investment group.

The status of your members, as respectable members of the business community, will be of assistance when you seek to establish a line
of credit. This is an exciting means of accelerating your rate of growth.

Investing as an Individual

But investment groups may not be your cup of tea. There's much
to be said for entering the field individually. Keep in mind that an
attorney will be involved in each mortgage transaction. That's basic.
You just cannot do it any other way. And you should not want to. The
attorney will guide and protect you and your money. At first, unless
you have already had some experience in the real estate field, he will

be your teacher as well as your legal counselor. As time progresses, and you have participated in a number of mortgage investments, you will find that the attorney is no longer your sole source of wisdom. You will become fully capable of valid evaluations yourself. You will never be able to draft a mortgage deed or a proper note, but you will be able to evaluate a prospective mortgagor, decide upon the amount you should invest, and the terms you should offer. The key here is the attorney.

Once again, a second mortgage proves to be a wondrous investment vehicle, for you choose your own attorney, a man whose sole and exclusive purpose is to protect and guide you—and the borrower usually pays the attorney's bill.

But, enough. We have dedicated an entire chapter to the individual investor — Chapter 5. All of the techniques necessary to create a successful mortgage investment program for the individual investor are set down in detail. Follow them, and the postman will wear out your front step bringing monthly checks from borrowers who have pledged their homes as security for the payment of your loan.

The Conservative Approach

Whatever approach you choose, follow it with the knowledge that second mortgage investing can be a conservative, yet lucrative, path to remarkable profits—profits that far exceed any other form of investment available to the average prudent man.

Yet, your funds will be invested so cautiously that this form of investment will exceed the conservative safety requirements of your neighborhood bank.

2

The Wonderful World
Of Mortgages

The Stability of a Mortgage ... Relative Quality of a Second
Mortgage ... Safety and High Earnings ... The Magic of Interest
... Home Improvement Loans, Charge Accounts, etc. ... "Low
Bank Rates" ... The True Annual Interest Rate Formula ... The
Broad 12 Per Cent Market ... The Benefits of Longer Terms ...
Bank Notes *vs.* Mortgage Notes ... Equity, the Magic Ingredient
... Viva Second Mortgages!

The Stability of a Mortgage

A mortgage is a pledge of property to a creditor as security for the
payment of a debt. When the debt is paid, the mortgage becomes void
and the creditor signs a release of mortgage.

Because the value of property, particularly residential real estate,
is relatively stable and rarely fluctuates to any great degree, savings
banks and loan associations place the largest portion of their assets in
mortgages, particularly residential mortgages. They know, and past
experience has verified, that no investment is more widely available,
more secure, or more capable of producing the higher income depositors demand.

Relative Quality of Second Mortgages

A second mortgage is an additional mortgage placed on property that has already been pledged. Because it is second in line, it sometimes carries the stigma of poor quality.

This value judgment is unfounded. A second mortgage can be of fine conservative investment quality, while a first mortgage can be a poor risk.

Consider two homes, one on Elm Street and the other on Western Avenue, each conservatively appraised at $18,000. The home on Elm Street carries a $14,400 first mortgage, while the Western Avenue home carries a first mortgage of $8,000 and a second mortgage of $3,500. Where would you prefer to have your money invested? In the first mortgage on Elm Street, or in the second mortgage on Western Avenue?

The adjectives "first" and "second," when applied to mortgages, are definitions, not evaluations. Prudently chosen, and this book will provide all the necessary management techniques, second mortgages are an incomparable investment vehicle.

Safety and High Earnings

Second mortgages are attractive for two reasons: Safety and high earnings. This combination is rare. High earnings are generally available only with high risks. Safety of capital usually results in low earnings.

The importance of safety is obvious. What does it profit a man, seeking a vigorous return of 10 per cent on his $3,500 investment, if he loses the $3,500? If Average Joe found one of his mortgages worthless, 60 per cent of the earnings of his full five-year investment plan would have been wiped out.

Safety is basic. Remember that. And second mortgages, following my Safety Formula and other techniques, make you as snug as a mortgage in a bank's vault. Snugger.

The Magic of Interest

High earnings? A constant return at a high interest rate does wondrous things. It takes 17-2/3 years for $100 to become $200 at 4 per cent a year, compounded annually. It takes only nine years at 8 per cent. At 10 per cent, your money doubles in just a bit more than seven years.

Let's take another step. Let's look at a regular savings program combined with the benefits of compound interest.

Average Joe financed his mortgage investments with weekly savings. If you do the same, and I assume you will, for regular investments accelerate the power of compound interest, the growth of your capital will astonish you.

For example, at 7 per cent return, your money will double in a shade over ten years. But if you invest $520 a year, or $10 a week, at the same 7 per cent, in ten years you will have amassed $7,685.60.

At a 10 per cent annual interest rate, with a $520 annual investment, your $5,200 total investment will be valued at $9,115.60 in ten years. In fifteen years you will have invested $7,800, and it will have grown to $18,174.00. In twenty years, your $10,200 will be $32,760!

Now that you have seen the astonishing results of each technique, compound interest on an initial investment and compound interest on a regular savings program, sit back a moment and think of what wondrous things could be achieved by combining the two—starting with an initial investment, and adding to it through a regular savings program.

Home Improvement Loans, Charge Accounts, etc.

Most of us know interest is something you earn when someone else uses your money, but our limited experience leads us to assume it has a range of only about three and a half per cent to six per cent. We know our savings account pays us somewhere within that range and that some of the higher-paying stock market investments earn about that amount.

But there's a great big world out there where people earn 8, 10, even 12 per cent on their money. And more.

The 6 per cent Home Improvement Loans available from your community bank are often within a fraction of 12 per cent true interest per annum. Your bank generally charges 6 per cent of the original amount of the loan for the entire life of the loan. Halfway through the life of that loan, the bank has half of its money back in the vault. Yet, you still pay 6 per cent on the full original amount of the loan. Statistically, their actual annual interest rate is a shade under 12 per cent true interest. Verbally, it's 6 per cent.

The "Instant Credit" check writing plan often carries a charge of 1 per cent a month, or 12 per cent true interest a year.

Many charge accounts are 1 per cent a month after the initial period. Some charge one and a half per cent, or 18 per cent true interest a year.

Small loan companies, specializing in personal loans, charge as much as 3 per cent a month on the first few hundred dollars, or 36 per cent true interest a year.

Pawnbrokers do pretty well, also.

Low Bank Rates

The prevalent theory is that the least expensive source of borrowed money is the local bank. This is often true, particularly when your loan is a personal loan calling for a single lump sum payment and carrying a true interest rate. But the loan form most commonly used by the public is a personal installment loan carrying monthly payments of principal and interest and a higher interest rate.

A two thousand dollar, 24-month personal installment loan at a local bank currently calls for the repayment of $2,298.85. The first monthly payment is $90.85. The remaining twenty-three monthly payments are $96.00 each.

That rate is 12.5 per cent per annum—pretty high for low.

It is true that a bank loan, carrying a true interest rate of almost 13 per cent per annum is available without any further cost. That is, no attorney's fees or recording costs are involved. To the extent that these costs exceed the total monthly advantages enjoyed by second mortgage debtors, bank loans are less costly.

A 10 per cent true interest second mortgage carries payments of $92.29 for twenty-four months, or a total of $2,214.96. Compared with the current rate for bank loans in my community, the gross mortgage savings would be $83.89.

Should the true interest rate be a high 12 per cent, the twenty-four payments of $94.15 would total $2,259.60. The installment loans lose again. This time by $39.25.

The True Annual Interest Rate Formula

To determine the true annual interest rate of an installment loan or an installment plan contract, use the following formula:

$$T = \frac{2\ M\ L}{B(N+1)}$$

T = True annual interest rate
M = Number of payment periods in one year (if monthly, 12; if weekly, 52)
L = Total interest paid in dollars during the life of the loan
B = Initial loan balance
N = Total number of payments to be made

The Broad 12 Per Cent Market

The public has been paying 12 per cent and more for many, many forms of the money it borrows, and is mathematically and financially conditioned to paying that rate. Loans are rarely verbalized with mathematical precision, however. "Six per cent" home improvement loans and "low bank rates" are the common approaches.

The frank admission that second mortgages cost 1 per cent a month on the declining balance, or 12 per cent a year, is often met with a pained expression.

Repeatedly, debtors carrying bank loans, improvement loans, personal loans, or instant credit loans, are appalled at the prospect of paying interest of 10 or 12 per cent a year. They are genuinely appalled. The reality of the interest rates they are paying their bankers or merchants eludes them completely.

A short discussion soon clears the air, but it's a cruel thing to do, exploding the 6 per cent myth or the fabled generosity of the neighborhood banker. Verbal interest rates are so much lower than their mathematical counterparts, and so much more comforting.

The Benefits of Longer Terms

One towering advantage of second mortgage financing as against personal bank loans is the longer term the mortgage investor is willing to grant.

A thousand dollar two-year loan, at a true 10 per cent annual rate, carries payments of $46.15 a month. Extending the payments over a three-year period cuts the monthly cost to $32.37. In four years, the monthly payments drop to $25.37, and in five years they become $21.25.

If the loan is for $2,000, the difference between a 24-month loan at $92.29 a month and a five-year loan at $42.50 a month can spell the difference between assuming a debt far beyond the borrower's ability to repay and undertaking one he can readily manage.

Second mortgages provide many other advantages to the borrower, the most dramatic of which is outlined in Chapter 4.

But let's get back to the mortgage investor.

I have not written this book to convince borrowers of the value of second mortgages. Each year, hundreds of thousands of people throughout these United States give second mortgages their vote of confidence by signing deeds and notes.

Bank Notes *vs.* Mortgage Notes

As an investor, which would you prefer to hold, the bank's $1,200 note or a $1,200 second mortgage?

Forget status. The banker, lending other people's money at 12.5 per cent per annum, is a public benefactor. The mortgage investor, lending his own money at 8, or 10, or 12 per cent per annum, is a money-lender. You'll never gain the banker's prestige.

Let's look at the investments themselves.

The banker lends money on credit rating, character, and past experience. But you add one more factor—equity in real estate. Your money is available only to a smaller group than the banker seeks. Those who pass his test must pass another one for you. Given a good credit rating, sterling character, and a healthy past, you still ask: Do they own sufficient equity in a parcel of real estate to secure my loan and insure its repayment?

Equity, the Magic Ingredient

Equity is the magic ingredient. Equity is the loan protection we seek, the comfort and security we solicit.

Ask the man in the street if he owns his home, and he will nod affirmatively with a warm smile.

Not so. Not so at all. The man in the street owns but a small portion of his home. The bank or insurance company holding the mortgage stands right up at the head of the line.

The "owner" gets what's left. And if the taxes haven't been paid, or the sewer or sidewalk assessments haven't been met, or there's an attachment or two, then the "owner" stands still farther back in line. And he still gets only what's left.

That's a good definition of equity: What's left.

Let's say you paid $20,000 for your home back in 1956. Your mortgage then was $16,000. Since then, it's been paid down to $13,150, and the value of the property has risen to $21,500. When you bought the house in 1956, your equity was $4,000, the difference between the $20,000 value of the property and the $16,000 mortgage. Since then, the equity has risen to $8,350, the difference between the current $21,500 property value and the current $13,150 mortgage balance.

	1956
Purchase Price (Market Value)	$20,000
Mortgage	-16,000
Equity	$ 4,000

	Today
Market Value	$21,500
Mortgage	-13,150
Equity	$ 8,350

This equity, or what is left for the owner after he sells his property and pays all the debts and liens outstanding against his title to the property, is the cushion that protects your mortgage investment.

The equity is also the basis for the clear superiority of a $1,200 private second mortgage over the bank's $1,200 note.

True, the bank may earn 12.5 per cent, but the private mortgage is a more conservative, more prudent, more sheltered investment. In a word, it is "secured." If the debtor defaults in his payments, the investor has an interest in a parcel of real estate towards which he can look for satisfaction of the debt.

This is particularly so if you follow my advice and apply the wondrous Safety Formula to each prospective mortgage investment. All of Chapter 10 is devoted to the details of this exciting, fool-proof key to earning high income with safety.

3

Realtors! Attorneys!
Accountants! Loan Officers!
Homeowners! Investors!

Shades of Sulfadiazine . . . Saving a Realtor's Sale . . . Purchase
Money Mortgage . . . Additional Income . . . The Key: An Attor-
ney's Skills . . . The Accountant, Source of Financial Counsel . . .
Client Seeks Additional Capital . . . Client Seeks to Invest Cash
. . . The Mortgage Loan Officer's Interview . . . The Growing
Private Mortgage Field . . . Homeowners, Wake Up . . . Patterns
of Mortgage Reduction . . . Using an Asset . . . Investors' Land of
Opportunity

Shades of Sulfadiazine

Second mortgages are a commercial wonder drug.

They have saved more debtors, rescued more eager home purchase
prospects, liberated more entombed assets, and extricated more investors than sulfadiazine.

No business counselor or real estate advisor can properly guide
his clients without a working knowledge of second mortgage techniques. No homeowner or investor can adequately plan his future
without insight into the remarkable advantages second mortgages
offer.

Saving a Realtor's Sale

Many a sale is lost when a prospective purchaser lacks the necessary cash. If the seller demands all cash and will not offer the buyer a purchase money mortgage to help cover the difference between the sales price of the house and the money the buyer has available through the bank's mortgage and his own cash, an increasing number of agents provide, or recommend, second mortgage financing to save the sale—and their commission.

Let's back-track. A seller agrees, instead of taking $20,000 in cash for his house, to accept $16,000 in cash and a mortgage to him of $4,000. The buyer then approaches a bank and negotiates an 80 per cent mortgage. Eighty per cent of the $20,000 purchase price is $16,000, the amount of cash the seller seeks. This particular buyer can then move in without investing any of his own cash. He will have, however, two mortgages as encumbrances against clear title to his new home, the first to the local savings and loan association, and the second to the seller.

Purchase Money Mortgages

This second mortgage, extended by the seller to the purchaser in order to secure the unpaid portion of the purchase price, is known as a purchase money mortgage. Because it is a means by which the owner is able to sell his home, and because he is usually eager to sell, the interest rate is generally no greater than that in the first mortgage. Low-interest rate purchase money mortgages are not investment vehicles; they are sales techniques, and thus beyond the coverage of this text.

The prior owner may be willing to accept only a $2,000 purchase money mortgage. In that case, the buyer of the $20,000 home with a $16,000 mortgage will need $2,000 in cash as well as the first and purchase money second mortgages.

Variations are endless. If an $18,000 house brings only a $12,000 bank mortgage, and the owner offers a $3,000 purchase money second mortgage, $3,000 in cash will be necessary to successfully conclude the purchase.

The owner may refuse to offer a purchase money mortgage. In that event, if the prospect has only $4,000 in cash, a $2,000 second mortgage can close the sale.

The point is, no real estate agent can claim competence without a thorough knowledge of this vast second mortgage field.

Certainly, he cannot perceive the techniques of resuscitation that can revive a dying sale.

Nor can he create his own sources of emergency secondary financing without a working knowledge of the wonders of second mortgage financing.

Every agent worth his salt knows people blessed with a surplus of cash seeking likely investment vehicles. Generally, they approach the agent with pleas for a "good piece of investment property." These people can become eager and continuing sources of private "save the sale" second mortgages if the agent understands the philosophy and techniques of this investment area well enough to adequately present them to the potential investor.

Additional Income

Some agents have created a sufficient demand for these by-products of real estate transactions to sell them on a commission basis to their eager sources of surplus capital. Two per cent is a common commission fee. Thus, a $1,500 second mortgage earns $30 for the agent.

The point is, if investors are willing to pay some agents for the privilege, you should have no trouble creating your own stable of "save the sale" investors to whom you would offer opportunities gratis.

The Key: An Attorney's Skills

No one is more vital to a successful private second mortgage investment program than a competent attorney.

The single most attractive aspect of the entire program, the security of the pledge of property to insure payment of the note, can be properly and safely created only through the skills of an attorney-at-law.

Most attorneys are thoroughly conversant with the techniques of buying or selling a house, and while counseling such a transaction, have developed a working familiarity with mortgages, generally first mortgages, to be sure, but mortgages nevertheless.

The techniques of second mortgage financing differ not a smidgen, except as to the more generous interest rate of the second mortgage.

An increasing number of clients, some with small sums, some with sizable amounts, are becoming aware of the remarkable second mortgage investment field. The idea of investing in mortgages remains just a theory until an attorney creates the documents that give it life.

A growing army of investors is beating an ever-widening path to attorneys' doors, asking to be led through the field of mortgage investment.

Every necessary form, every advisable check list, every valuable technique, is detailed in this book.

Because of the education an attorney has received and the experiences he has encountered, the information contained here will enable him to lead with competence, advise with insight, and counsel with confidence.

The Accountant, Source of Financial Counsel

The accountant plays a vital role in the growth of his client's enterprises and financial well-being.

Yet, there are areas in which even skilled accountants are in need of further education.

There are two areas of major concern to the business or professional man that fall within the scope of this book. And in both areas the accountant well may be the prime counselor.

Client Seeks Additional Capital

First, the client needs additional capital. He has been in business at the same location for seven years and it is time to expand. Or he has need for new equipment. Or wants to take on a new line. Whatever the reason, he needs money. And although his credit is good, he is using it to the hilt now. Where can he turn?

One source is a local private mortgage investor. By securing secondary mortgage financing on his home, the client would be transforming the equity in his house, a passive asset, into an active financial tool. Chances are, the client's mortgage has been substantially reduced during the passing years, and further, chances are that the value of his home has increased as land values rose and improvements were added.

Whether a second mortgage is the precise answer or not, is not the point. The point is, it is an alternative. A possibility to be explored. Too many financial advisors who should know better, overlook it completely.

They rarely overlook mortgage refinancing; yet, as Chapter 4 will show, a second mortgage is vastly superior and results in remarkable savings.

Client Seeks to Invest Excess Cash

Second, the client has excess cash and wonders where to invest it. As popular as second mortgage investing may be, there are still professionals whose lack of understanding of the potentials of prudent private mortgages leads to disapproval of them as an investment vehicle.

To be sure, there are instances when mortgage investments would not be advisable.

But mortgage investment is as secure, flexible, marketable (yes, I said marketable—see Chapter 20) and profitable as anything the client will have readily available.

Unless the accountant has an understanding of the private mortgage investment field, he cannot adequately advise those clients who are either seeking cash or seeking an investment vehicle.

The Mortgage Loan Officer's Interview

The prospective purchaser has seen the property he wants, the price is a bit high, but it's what he wants, and worth the few dollars more.

But he certainly can't pay all cash, and the existing mortgage is so low he'd need a fortune.

His only chance is getting a new mortgage from a bank or insurance company, a high mortgage.

He talks to the loan officer and outlines his problem. One of two things will now happen. Either the loan officer will click his tongue, sadly shake his head from side to side, all the while sympathizing that the most he can offer is a $20,000 mortgage—or the interviewer will brighten a bit and say, "We can make $20,000 of it available to you. You have $5,000 in ready cash. Why don't you consider a private second mortgage for the balance?"

The difference between the dusty, unrealistic approach and the shiny, realistic one is a new mortgage for the bank's portfolio. One bank officer, confined by the rigors of formalized thinking, completely discourages a potential mortgagor. The other not only goes a long way towards selling his bank's mortgage, but earns himself a grateful, and steady, client.

I've met both types. Haven't you?

I've met realistic bankers who not only suggest the possibilities of a second mortgage, but also recommend reputable investors.

Incidentally, the reflex of suggesting refinancing to meet a temporary financial need should be carefully re-examined in the light of the statistics of Chapter 4.

The Growing Private Mortgage Field

Finally, no loan officer can claim competence in the vigorous and ever-changing field of finance without an up-to-date understanding of the private mortgage investment field. The *Wall Street Journal* recently used its front page to report the rapid growth, wide activity, and increasing number of second mortgage lenders. It reported that General Electric Company and Westinghouse Electric Corporation have joined a growing parade of large national corporations which now employ a form of second mortgage financing.

A recent Sunday edition of the *New York Times* used the front page of its real estate section to report: "Short Term Loan Useful in Realty. Interim Financing Often the Way to a Successful Deal."

A first mortgage is rarely the full solution to an investment opportunity.

When available cash is limited, and purchase money mortgages are either unavailable or insufficient, a second mortgage may well enable a mortgagor to pluck a juicy plum, and a loan department to negotiate a satisfying mortgage.

Homeowners, Wake Up!

The enormous number of home owners who do not realize that their steadily diminishing mortgage balance represents an asset of considerable value and virility is appalling. Sadder still is the homeowner who recognizes the value of his expanding equity but does not know how to use the asset properly to realize the funds it potentially represents.

One of the joys of home ownership, quite apart from the privilege of manicuring the lawn and fertilizing the yews, is the reduction of the mortgage balance by a portion of the monthly mortgage payment.

In the early months, the reductions begin microscopically and grow almost grudgingly until they become merely small. With the passage of years, however, the diminution of principal accelerates and creates an inversely proportionate accelerated reduction in interest due. As one increases, the other declines. Eventually, in a process not unlike Chinese water torture or soil erosion, the mortgage balance suddenly succumbs. The portion of the monthly payment that is applied to principal eventually exceeds the interest payment. Some time thereafter, the mortgage balance is less than one-half its original size.

Patterns of Mortgage Reduction

Using a $15,000 twenty-year 6 per cent mortgage as an example, the pattern of reduction of the mortgage balance looks approximately like this:

Year	Total % Unpaid	Annual Reduction of Principal	Mortgage Balance
First year	97.3	$405	$14,595
Second	94.5	420	14,175
Third	91.5	450	13,725
Fourth	88.3	480	13,245
Fifth	84.9	510	12,735
Sixth	81.2	550	12,180
Seventh	77.4	570	11,610
Eighth	73.3	615	10,995
Ninth	69.0	645	10,350
Tenth	64.4	690	9,660

Year	Total % Unpaid	Annual Reduction of Principal	Mortgage Balance
Eleventh	59.6	720	8,940
Twelfth	54.4	780	8,160
Thirteenth	48.9	825	7,335
Fourteenth	43.1	870	6,465
Fifteenth	36.9	930	5,535
Sixteenth	30.3	990	4,545
Seventeenth	23.3	1,050	3,495
Eighteenth	15.9	1,110	2,385
Nineteenth	8.1	1,170	1,215

The monthly payment, covering principal and interest, is $107.47, or approximately $1,290 per annum. By the end of the ninth year, one-half of the annual mortgage payment, or $645, is applied towards reduction of the mortgage. Thereafter, the proportion increases.

Note that it is not until almost the thirteenth year that one-half of the twenty-year loan is repaid.

A twenty-five year, 6 per cent mortgage for $15,000 carries monthly payments of $96.65, or almost $1,160 per annum, and creates reduction figures approximately as follows:

Year	Total % Unpaid	Annual Reduction of Principal	Mortgage Balance
First	98.2	$270	$14,730
Second	96.3	285	14,445
Third	94.3	300	14,145
Fourth	92.2	315	13,830
Fifth	89.9	345	13,485
Sixth	87.5	360	13,125
Seventh	84.9	390	12,735
Eighth	82.2	405	12,330
Ninth	79.3	435	11,895
Tenth	76.2	465	11,430
Eleventh	73.0	480	10,950
Twelfth	69.5	525	10,425
Thirteenth	65.9	540	9,885
Fourteenth	62.0	585	9,300
Fifteenth	57.8	630	8,670

Year	Total % Unpaid	Annual Reduction of Principal	Mortgage Balance
Sixteenth	53.4	660	8,010
Seventeenth	48.8	690	7,320
Eighteenth	43.8	750	6,570
Nineteenth	38.6	780	5,790
Twentieth	33.0	840	4,950
Twenty-First	27.1	885	4,065
Twenty-Second	20.8	945	3,120
Twenty-Third	14.1	1,005	2,115
Twenty-Fourth	7.0	1,065	1,050

At the fourteenth year, one-half of the $1,160 annual mortgage payment is applied to reduction of the mortgage principal.

Just before the seventeenth year, the loan balance has been cut in half.

Using an Asset

No homeowner should spend years of his life tediously laying monthly sacrifices at the altar of his mortgage without comprehending that he is doing more than earning an income tax saving for interest paid and a reduction in his mortgage balance. His diminishing mortgage is an asset as real and as valued as government bonds or a savings account.

The key question is how does a homeowner, with a child to educate or a wife in a hospital, realize the value of that asset? How does he turn his increasing equity in his home into cash without selling the home?

Undoubtedly, the most popular and most widely recommended technique for raising funds of that sort is refinancing the mortgage, rewriting it for at least the original amount. If his $15,000 twenty-five year, 6 per cent mortgage were eleven years old, he would gross approximately $5,050.

Don't do it. Read the next chapter, Chapter 4. Refinancing is a foolish, extravagant, inadvisable technique.

On the other hand, he could use his increased equity as security for a loan.

That is what this book is all about. There is just no comparison. Rewriting the mortgage is totally inferior as a fund-raising technique.

A comprehension of the techniques of borrowing money, using real estate equity as security without disturbing the bank's mortgage, will save the homeowner many, many thousands of dollars.

Investors' Land of Opportunity

An increasing number of citizens are aware of the need, and the joys, of creating supplemental income. In this affluent society, ski lodges, water skiing, power boats, or private planes are no longer the exclusive domain of the landed gentry. Young America wants a slice of the pie. Their parents do, too. Retired America no longer views the quiet years as a period of minimal existence. Dynamic living is today's criterion, not mere existence.

There are many standard forms for achieving a supplemental income. Common stocks, real estate, or franchising, to name a few. Have you heard of investing in futures in the scotch market? Or buying rolls of current coins for their appreciation in value? Antiques have their partisans, as do paintings, or first editions.

Most investment areas have already been staked out by people with awesome skills, ready capital, and religious fervor. And the investments are relatively exotic. They call for a degree of dedication, a surplus of cash, and an encyclopedic grasp of austere skills that are far beyond the reach of most of us.

So what do you do? Mumble to yourself and wait for Social Security? Plunge into treacherous waters already cluttered with frantically gyrating investors? No.

Read a while and discover a new land of opportunity. Second mortgages. From afar you'd never guess the potentials it contains. Few travelers head that way.

Those who do, learn to love it.

4

The Startling
Homeowner Benefits

Homeowner Needs Cash ... Refinancing a Seven-Year-Old Mortgage ... 12 Per Cent Is Cheaper than 6 Per Cent ... The Odds Are Six to One ... Chart ... The Startling Statistics ... The Repercussions of Higher Interest ... Confirming Opinions ... Why People Borrow

Homeowner Needs Cash

It was seven years ago that Murray Mortgagor bought his home. It cost him $12,000. His bank supplied a twenty-five-year, 4½ per cent mortgage in the amount of $9,600, and Murray contributed $2,400 in cash.

Since then, by carefully mailing a check every month, Murray has lowered his mortgage to $7,888, and increased his equity to $3,112, based on the original value of the property.

But Murray has a problem. He needs cash.

Why? Any one of a million reasons. Doctor bills. College costs. A new car. An extended vacation. A consolidation of existing debts.

Murray needs $3,000.

Refinancing a Seven-Year-Old Mortgage

He decides that the wisest way to raise $3,000 would be to refinance his home. That is, to place a new mortgage on his home based on the new value of the property, use the new mortgage funds to pay off the balance of the old mortgage, and keep what's left for his own needs.

Because his home is now worth $14,000, a local savings and loan association would offer an $11,200 mortgage, or 80 per cent of its value.

There are expenses to be paid, of course. There's an application fee of $25.00, a credit report cost of $4.00, attorney's fees of $100, and recording costs of $19. Thus, rather than $11,200, there is actually only $11,052 available to the mortgagor.

Murray's existing mortgage has a balance of $7,888. There is often a penalty for prepayment of a mortgage. One per cent of the original principal is a common penalty, and would cost Murray $96. But we will not apply any penalty in analyzing the costs of refinancing.

Using the $11,052 available from the new $11,200 mortgage after mortgage closing costs are deducted, and applying it to the existing mortgage balance of $7,888, Murray will be able to retain $3,164 after refinancing his home at 6 per cent interest per year.

But this approach is infinitely more costly than second mortgaging. As a matter of fact, where bona fide second mortgages are available, I cannot conceive of any conscientious financial adviser advocating refinancing.

Twelve Per Cent Is Cheaper Than Six Per Cent

The startling fact is that a $3,250 second mortgage, even at a 12 per cent annual interest rate, would have saved Murray $6,292 when compared with refinancing his home at a 6 per cent annual interest rate.

That's right. A second mortgage would have saved him $6,292!

At 12 per cent, or twice as high an interest rate, a second mortgage of $3,250 would call for payments of $72.30 a month for five years, or total payments of $4,338 over the life of the loan. The $3,250 would result in cash proceeds of $3,151 after costs of ninety-nine dollars. When the cash proceeds are deducted from the total monthly payments for the five years, the net cost of a 12 per cent mortgage is $1,187.

The Odds Are Six to One

On the other hand, Murray had 18 years remaining of a 25-year, four and a half per cent, $9,600 mortgage. The balance of his payments would have been $53.36 a month for 216 months, or $11,525.76 during the remaining life of his original mortgage.

In order to get $3,164 in cash, Murray refinanced his home at $11,200 for the same period of time as the original mortgage, 25 years, and at the current rate of interest, six per cent. His new monthly payments were $73.89 for 300 months, or a total of $22,167 during the remaining life of his new mortgage.

His new mortgage, then, would cost him $10,642 more than the remaining payments due on his original mortgage and would produce only the $3,164 in cash that he sought.

The net cost of the $3,164 cash proceeds would be $7,478, while a second mortgage would cost $1,186.

The staggering difference is $6,292. In this typical fact situation, refinancing costs more than six times the cost of a second mortgage.

Chart

REFINANCING

Proceeds:	Mortgage available	$11,200.00
	Closing costs	-148.00
		$11,052.00
	Pay-off of existing mortgage	$-7,888.00
	Cash available	$ 3,164.00
Cost:	New mortgage ($11,200, 6%, 25 years, $73.86 per month)	
	Monthly payments	$ 73.86
	Months remaining (25 years)	x300
	Total payments	$22,167.00
	Original mortgage ($9,600, 4-1/2%, 25 years, $53.36 per month)	
	Monthly payments	$ 53.36
	Months remaining	x216
	Total payments remaining	$11,525.76
	New mortgage	$22,167.00
	Original mortgage	-11,525.76
	Additional cost	$10,641.24
	Less resulting cash	-3,164.00
	Cost of resulting cash	$ 7,477.24

SECOND MORTGAGE

Proceeds:	Mortgage available	$ 3,250.00
	Closing costs	-99.00
	Cash available	$ 3,151.00
Cost:	($3,250, 12%, 5 years, $77.30 per month)	
	Monthly payments	$ 72.30
	Months remaining (5 years)	x60
	Total payments	$ 4,338.00
	Less resulting cash	-3,151.00
	Cost of resulting cash	$ 1,187.00

COMPARING COSTS

Refinancing	$ 7,477.24
Second mortgage	-1,187.00
	$ 6,290.24

Ratio:	Refinancing costs	$6.29
	Second mortgage costs	$1.19

The Startling Statistics

Why? Because Murray is replacing a four and a half per cent mortgage with a six per cent mortgage. The difference in cost for this one factor alone would be $7.08 a month for $8,000. Over a 25-year period, $7.08 a month amounts to $2,124.

The balance of $7,888, which was to be paid off in the 18 remaining years of the original mortgage, would now be stretched out over the 25 years of the new mortgage. Even at the same six per cent interest rate, $8,000 would cost $236.24 more if the payments are stretched out over 25 years than if they were computed in 18 years.

And finally, Murray was dealing with a considerably larger sum of mony. In place of a balance of $7,888, he undertook a new balance of $11,200, an increase of more than 40 per cent.

The second mortgage will win every time. Normal refinancing cannot compare, because it inevitably necessitates a higher interest rate than the current first mortgage carries, a longer term, and an increase in principal.

Whenever unusual circumstances change any of these factors, the costs of refinancing may not be as overwhelming—but they will still be considerably higher, almost without exception.

A second mortgage will temporarily increase the monthly mortgage payments to $117.27 in Murray's example, as against $73.89 for his new mortgage, or $43.38 more a month. Some poor souls just cannot manage an additional $10 a week, no matter how attractive the mathematics. They will be compelled by unhappy circumstances to forego the sizable saving over the long run for the minor saving of the near term.

The Repercussions of Higher Interest

Occasionally the refinancing interest rate will be only a bit higher than the original. Only one-half per cent? Although the difference per monthly payment is only $2.95 a month at $10,000, carried for the life of the loan one-half per cent costs the mortgagor $885.

Three-quarters of a per cent will cost an additional $1,338.

One percentage point difference in the interest rate, just one per cent, will cost $1,794 for the same amount of money.

In addition, minimizing one factor just isn't enough. After ten years, a 25-year mortgage rewritten for the original amount and the original term of years at an increase of only one half of one per cent interest will not cost a mere $885 over the 25-year life of the new mortgage.

The mortgagor had only 15 years remaining at, say five per cent. That is, 180 payments at $58.46, or a total balance of $10,522.80.

Rewriting for 25 years at the modestly higher interest rate means a monthly raise of only $2.95, or the $885 we discussed—but it also means continuing those payments for an additional 120 months at the higher rate, or an added expense of $7,369.20. The total additional cost is now $8,254.

The pitiful thing is that the mortgage reduction being refinanced, for which the cost will be $8,254, is only $2,610.

If refinancing costs are as low as $153, a cash balance of $2,457 will carry $5,797 in interest costs.

A $2,550 second mortgage at 12 per cent for five years, producing a net of $2,456, would cost $56.73 a month, for a total of $3,403, or $853 in interest costs, $4,944 cheaper than refinancing.

All of which leads us to a bit of advice. Given an existing mortgage old enough to produce a sizable sum through refinancing,

AND, if you can refinance at an interest rate somehow similar to the prevalent rate of years past,

AND, if you can refinance for a term of years equal to the years remaining under the old mortgage,

AND, if you can resist the temptation, or forego the need, to refinance at a sum based upon the new, appreciated value of the property in this era of rising realty values,

THEN, consider refinancing.

Confirming Opinions

Sylvia Porter, a nationally syndicated authority on economics and finance has discussed the trend toward mortgage refinancing for non-home purposes. It's "sweeping the country in recent years." It breaks "a fundamental rule of sound finance by borrowing long to buy short."

Dr. M. R. Neifeld, a nationally respected expert on consumer credit, in an issue of *Personal Finance Law,* illustrated the extraordinary costs of mortgage refinancing by comparing it with a short-term loan. His illustration showed that mortgage refinancing costs above five times more. As Neifeld says, "The easy appeal of refinancing a home mortgage to obtain cash for non-home equity purposes glosses over the tremendous difference in interest costs."

Why People Borrow

It may interest you to know why people borrow. An analysis by one of the largest small loan organizations in the world indicates that the primary reason is consolidation of unpaid bills. "Pay all the bills in one swoop, relieve yourself of the burden of being in debt to a large number of people, renew your credit, eliminate the agonies of writing a large number of checks each month, and have only one creditor to pay each month."

Borrowing to buy or repair an automobile is next, followed by vacationing, medical, dental, and hospital bills, clothing, assisting relatives, buying appliances or furniture, taxes, home maintenance, equipment, insurance, moving, a new business, repaying loans, education, fuel, rent, funeral expenses, and a large miscellaneous grouping.

There are some surprises. Vacationing is third. Taxes are eighth. Education is fifteenth. Interesting.

5

Getting Started
As An Individual Investor

Philosophizing...Realism...Exploring the World of Finance...Use Money...Finding a Realtor...Friends and Advertisements...Business Cards...Other Techniques...Mortgage Brokers...Newspaper Display Ads...The Yellow Pages...Tailor the Costs to Your Pocketbook...Independence...A Word about Newspapers.

Philosophizing

Forgive me, but I must take a moment to philosophize.

It seems to have become a contemporary tradition to live within a nickel of our income. Whatever comes in, less taxes, goes out in an everflowing stream.

Ten years ago, you would have chuckled about owning two houses, one a vacation retreat. Could you have imagined owning an electric toothbrush, garbage disposal, electric blanket, automatic dishwasher, electric carving knife, air-conditioner, color television, or power lawn mower? Never.

Today, I'll bet the majority of you reading these words use at least four of those exotic appliances with regularity.

The steady stream of seductive symbols of the "good life" keeps our check book humming—and though our personal income continues to rise, the end of the year finds us saving no more than we did before the income increase.

The remarkable spending skills we have developed are based largely upon a warm sense of confidence in the future. It will be good, and our place in the scheme of things will be better.

The future? Social Security benefits are rising. Medical care for the aged is expanding. The company's raised the pension plan again. By golly, things look good.

Realism

At the risk of being called a spoil sport, I would like to suggest that a responsible spouse, a considerate parent, and a realistic citizen must take tomorrow into account.

Your parents take ill. There's no bonus this year. Your son's college raises the tuition rates again. The plant stops needing overtime.

What do you do?

Chances are you scurry and scramble, borrow a bit from the Credit Union, or see the local bank about a personal loan, and berate yourself for losing control.

I have a much better idea.

Develop a hobby. Raise money for fun and profit. Learn what money is all about. Is interest only what you pay everyone else? How can you get on the other side of the desk?

I am not suggesting that you forsake your garden trowel or your putter—nor do I imply that you should forego taking the wife to the local steak house or standing a round for the boys at the annual outing. No.

Everything in moderation. Take a few hours of your time. Take 10 per cent of your income; less, if necessary.

Exploring the World of Finance

Developing the skills to earn a second income can be an exhilarating experience. It will open new vistas, new frontiers. The world of finance is as lively as a pennant race, as challenging as a kick-off run back, and as satisfying as the first day of the fishing season.

The world of finance starts in your own home town. It starts with personal loans. It picks up speed with mortgages, and roars full throttle into property ownership. There are side excursions into Stock Market Sound and the Bay of Bonds.

Yet all have a common golden thread. Finance. Using money to make money is the first step. Most of us use all of our money for purchases.

Why all?

Have you ever stopped to analyze why savings institutions advertise so extensively and sometimes offer depositors attractive gift premiums? They sell money. Like any good merchant, their profits depend on buying at wholesale prices (savings account interest) and selling at substantially higher prices (mortgage, home improvement, automobile, and personal loans).

Does that give you a clue?

Use Money

Take a small percentage of your income and use it to make money. Within a short period of time you will have learned the skills of mortgage investment. You will have developed an understanding of the financial machinery that you and your neighbors have kept greased all these gay, blind years. You will have glimpsed a truth that can mean a glorious second income and a comfortable retirement. Money, properly managed, begets money, and the more it multiplies, the more it multiples.

It will be only a matter of time before you find the ultimate truth, the key to the palace gates—other people's money. The banks do it.

As a matter of fact, the banks will help you join in the fun. Nothing will please them more, when your skills and your financial status reflecting those skills warrant, than to lend you 4 per cent money (their cost for money deposited in savings accounts) for 6 per cent (the normal cost a sophisticated borrower pays for borrowing money deposited in savings accounts). See Chapter 18.

I assure you that you will find the world of second mortgage investment as exciting as any hobby you might choose, and undoubtedly more rewarding.

I have already discussed the initial financing. A ten-dollar-a-week program and fifteen hundred dollars is enough to start you on your way. It will finance your first mortgage investment.

Of course, as is always the case where money is concerned, the minimum is fine, but a great deal is better.

Whatever the amount circumstances permit you to start with, add faithfully by weekly savings. Faithfully. Weekly.

If you will forgive the pun—the savings might even be weakly. Do what you can. Always keep in mind that investments of any kind should be undertaken only when your insurance portfolio is adequate and your savings are sufficient to meet your family's needs.

You have the money. Now we find clients.

Finding a Realtor

Take out your community's telephone book. Turn to the yellow pages under "Real Estate Agents." These gentlemen are the key to the local real estate market. They introduce purchasers to sellers. They are a commercial marriage bureau. Their imagination, experience, and sales ability are the catalytic agents that create the exchanges of ownership we call the real estate market.

Very often they find a potential purchaser who is eager to buy a $25,000 home. A mortgage of $20,000 is available, and the potential purchaser has scraped together $4,000 in cash. One thousand dollars will be necessary to complete the transaction.

If someone were to provide the cash, the agent would earn a commission, the seller would get his full price, and the buyer's wife would have her "dream house."

Tell the real estate agent you have $1,500 available for a second mortgage investment.

If he is a competent agent, he will eagerly take your name and address and call when he has a potential sale that lacks $1,500 for completion. You will have planted a seed.

Repeat the call to other agents. Spread the news.

Friends and Advertisements

Your friends and acquaintances are a fine source of mortgage leads. Mention your interest in a mortgage investment. You will be amazed at the number who will pass the news of their "financial contact" to potential mortgagors. It becomes a source of pride to many people to casually comment that should anyone need fifteen hundred dollars, they have a friend astute enough—and rich enough—to have the money available.

Try the newspapers. A simple classified ad will cost less than a dollar a day. For a minimum of ten words you can tell the whole story:

> LOANS IMMEDIATELY AVAILABLE. $1,500
> COSTS ONLY $33.37 MONTHLY. 989-1234

Use your own phone number rather than a post office box or a mailing address. The telephone will ring often, and most of the callers will not meet your standards, but the calls will give you the experience you need in learning to evaluate mortgage opportunities.

Within a few weeks you will have developed the knack of asking the right questions, seeing through evasive answers, applying those investigation techniques detailed in Chapter 9, and using our remarkable Safety Formula set out in Chapter 10.

Business Cards

You might invest approximately $6.50 to have a hundred business cards printed, or a few dollars more for five hundred. A small investment, but one that adds an aura of stability to the position you have chosen for yourself.

First, choose a name. Shall it be your own?

JOHN B. DOE
123 OAK STREET
HOMETOWN, PENNSYLVANIA

Mortgage Loans   Telephone 989-1234

Or perhaps you would prefer to use a business name:

CAPITAL INVESTMENTS

ARROW MORTGAGES

In that case your business card might then read:

CAPITAL INVESTMENTS
123 OAK STREET
HOMETOWN, PENNSYLVANIA

TELEPHONE: 989-1234

Mortgage Loans   John B. Doe

Either approach is valid. Your choice should be made after evaluating your community, your contacts, and your own intuition.

In any case, any neat card is preferable to none.

For an additional few dollars you can substantially increase the impact and usefulness of your business card. Incorporate the interest rates prevailing in your community. Draw up a payment schedule and print it on the rear of your card:

MONTHLY PAYMENTS

	$1,500	$2,000	$2,500	$3,000
3 yrs.	48.41	64.54	80.67	96.81
4 yrs.	38.05	50.73	63.41	76.09
5 yrs.	31.88	42.50	53.12	63.75

Experience shows that including the payment schedule transforms the card from "just another one of those business things" into an interesting item that many people keep in a handy place.

Other Techniques

Depending on the size of your community, you might try mailing an announcement to local realtors. Include your business card.

Try attorneys and accountants, too. They often come into contact with people in need of additional funds.

Remind the realtors that using your cash might result in saving a sale and protecting his commission.

Suggest to the attorney that if he finds you a borrower, you would be happy to hire him to draft the necessary documents, check the title, and supervise the closing.

Advise the accountant that some of his business clients could earn far in excess of the second mortgage interest charge by discounting their bills. Not only would they benefit financially, but their credit rating would soar.

If the realtors' reception is cool, you might consider offering him a commission for finding you a customer. Commissions vary from state to state, just as permissible interest rates do, but 2 or 3 per cent of the mortgage amount should be within range.

Mortgage Brokers

If you are fortunate, your community may have a resident mortgage broker, a man who earns his livelihood creating and catering to the private mortgage market.

In exchange for a reasonable commission, discussed above, a mortgage broker will introduce eager borrowers to willing lenders. His services include procuring a credit report, appraising the property, providing photographs of the premises, and sharing his evaluation of the quality of the prospective investment.

Assuming that he is a sincere businessman, a man of integrity, no one could be of more benefit to a neophyte investor. Coupled with a competent attorney of your own choosing, you ride into battle armed to the teeth.

Approach with a degree of caution, however. The broker's income is dependent upon his ability to sell his products. A sharp operator might exaggerate the value of the property in order to present a rosy picture, and close a sale.

Generally, I think you will find the majority of brokers are more concerned with developing a loyal clientele. Knowing that clients result from successful investments, most brokers will handle you with caution and concern.

Your greatest problem will be convincing him that you really will accept only conservative mortgages that meet the standards of our Safety Formula. His experience may well be that, as long as his appraisal equals the balance of both mortgages, his customers are happy. Don't permit him to change your standards in this vital area.

If you develop a relationship with a competent broker, you should find your knowledge increasing as your portfolio grows. Never hesitate to ask questions, to pose problems, or to modestly challenge his judgment. A good broker will welcome the exchange.

Newspaper Display Ads

Newspaper ads are productive. I do not mean just the classified pages discussed earlier. They often have limited impact, generally reaching only those people who are consciously seeking funds—and those people who are knowledgeable enough to know that the classified pages contain sections such as "Loans" or "Mortgages."

This is not to say that classified ads are worthless. Quite the contrary. They are low in cost. If your first step into the mortgage market is a limited one, if you are seeking to place only one or two mortgages, classified advertisements are a fine buy. Why use a bomb to get a mosquito?

If, on the other hand, you have a sizable amount of money and hope to place a number of mortgages, a display advertisement in the main body of your local newspaper might be the most effective and the most productive medium.

A display ad will do more than find customers. As noted in earlier comments about classified ads, if you use your own telephone number, rather than a post office box or other mailing address, it will educate you. The calls in reply will give you the experience you need in evaluating mortgage opportunities.

Because the display ad reaches more people, the number of calls will be substantially greater and your education will be accelerated.

Here is a sample display ad that has proven successful:

HOMEOWNERS

IMMEDIATE CASH AVAILABLE

	3 years	4 years	5 years
$1,500	$48.41	$38.05	$31.88
$2,000	$64.54	$50.73	$42.50

No application or appraisal fees
Confidential and speedy service

HARTFORD CAPITAL FUND — Phone 567-2345

The Yellow Pages

You might consider a business listing in the Yellow Pages under the heading "Loans" or "Mortgages."

I prefer "Loans." Those potential second mortgagors who need funds are rarely sophisticated enough to realize that the legal technique through which the funds are made available would be a mortgage. Use the "Loans" section. It's the first place someone using the directory would look.

Tailor the Costs to Your Pocketbook

The basic point is that you can get started easily by word of mouth, without incurring more than a very modest telephone bill.

True, it may be a slow technique. If it is too slow, and you don't mind spending a few dollars, print some business cards.

The next step up the expense ladder would be the classified ads. Then a mailing, display ads in the local newspaper, or a mortgage broker.

A Yellow Page listing should not be considered until you have at least a full year, and considerable capital, behind you.

Independence

Using a broker creates one problem worthy of comment at this early stage.

If you limit your procurement program exclusively to the services of a broker, and undertake none of the other techniques we have discussed, you will find that you never achieve independence. As the years pass, only your broker and his clients will be aware that you exist.

If you utilize the services of a broker during your early years, consider incorporating one or two personal techniques as well.

It may not be possible for you to be initially independent. It would not be wise to be perpetually dependent.

A Word about Newspapers

Before passing on to other items, it is important to recognize that newspaper advertising should not be considered a one-shot technique.

Individual ads generally do not bring in potential mortgagors. Of course, isolated eager borrowers will respond. But a consistent flow of inquiries stems from repetition of the ad. Seeing it the first or second time strikes a tiny bell. Unless the reader is consciously seeking a loan, it will do little more than register tentatively. As he notices it from time to time, his recognition grows. Finally, after weighing his pile of bills against his checking account balance, he remembers seeing an ad about borrowing money. "The payments were less than those personal loan companies. Wish I could remember where I saw it." Naturally, he never expected to use it. But you can bet he will be looking for it now. The next time he sees it, he tears it out, calls your number—and you may have a new client.

6

Consider Organizing A Group

Why? ... Three Simple Steps ... Look, Spot, Look. See the
Money ... Develop a Good Habit ... Expand Your Contacts ...
Group Benefits ... Beware the Adventurer ... Fie on Modesty

Why

You may not be the type to go at it alone. Perhaps you have no
time for the interviews, the advertising, the investigation, and the
administration. Perhaps you are so modest you refuse to believe that
your skills or your inclinations will enable you to undertake the
management of a mortgage portfolio. Perhaps you are the gregarious
type. You see the remarkable potential clearly enough, but you know
that you would be far happier sharing the excitement and the income
with a congenial group of like-minded investors. Perhaps your re-
sources are limited, and though you agree that the conservative approach is the proper one, you would like to combine with others. After
all, a group of investors will enable you to enjoy the excitement of a
more extensive portfolio than your personal financial circumstances
would permit.

For whatever reason you choose to create a group, the experience
will be simple, educational, and very rewarding.

Three Simple Steps

The approach is simple. It involves only enthusiasm, preparation, and people. Of the three, two are my responsibility.

I hope to generate the enthusiasm—and I intend to provide all the necessary information, to assure that you are fully prepared.

Step One. Read this book thoroughly. Understand it. Think it through. Know it well enough, and believe in it deeply enough, to be able to present its recommendations with genuine enthusiasm. Enthusiasm generates interest. And knowledgeable leadership generates confidence.

Step Two. Call a few friends. If circumstances permit, make it a luncheon meeting. Wherever possible, include an attorney, an accountant, a realtor, and a banker. This caliber of man will not be interested in taking a wild fling. He will appreciate, though, being invited to participate in the formation of a conservative investment group capable of earning an uncommonly high return. Discuss our Safety Formula, our investigative safeguards, and our philosophy of prudence.

And discuss who else you plan to call. It is imperative that those involved respect and enjoy the company of one another. If two of your first contacts do not get along well, drop one of them.

Sharing the names of those you intend to invite will be a strong indication of the level of quality you are seeking to obtain. Mentioning a well-respected attorney and a highly regarded Certified Public Accountant will earn the respect of the realtor or banker you hope will join the team. They will be more likely to accept your invitation if they feel you are pointing towards a high level of professional competence.

If your circle does not include an attorney, accountant, realtor, or banker, don't fret. Take a few moments in a quiet corner and think. You must have friends who know people in those professional areas. Call them. They may be an assistant buyer in the local department store or an insurance salesman. Call them. And call anyone else who has acquaintances in professional circles.

Don't just tell them that you want to form a group to invest in second mortgages. Spell it out. Create respect for the conservative approach you expect to follow and enthusiasm for the exciting potential for profit that it entails.

Then ask them for recommendations in the professions I've outlined.

Step Three. When you have six to ten people, people who promise
a congenial working relationship, people whose skills will enable your
group to take the first steps, stop.

Invite them to an exploratory meeting. A business office is preferable to a living room. It sets a professional tone, a no-nonsense
atmosphere. The more professional the tone of the office, the more
impact your initial planning session will have.

When your prospective charter members are assembled, present
your thoughts in detail.

There will be many questions. Anticipate them. Plan your presentation in advance. Have the necessary materials on hand—the regulations, the mortgage closing check list, the local statutes relating to
interest charges, etc. All of the basic information is included in this
book.

You might choose my table of contents as a guide, and present
your information as I have presented mine.

Whatever approach you take, be thorough. Your invitees may be
skeptical. At the very least, they will have many questions. A logical
approach will provide the answers as the questions arise—and gain
their respect.

Look, Spot, Look. See the Money

Creating an investment group benefits the individual members of
the group in many ways.

The benefits go beyond the mere advantages of earning a considerable income from your investments. The benefits involve the skills
you will develop, the excitement you will experience, the worthwhile
habits you will develop, and the wider circle of friends you will meet.

The use of money to make money is a common skill in some
quarters. Its techniques are unknown, however, to the vast majority of
people. Gaining a thorough working understanding of this one investment field—learning the value of credit reports, the availability of
bank loans, the impact of taxation, the potential of the local real estate
market—all of these are threads that run through innumerable investment areas. It will open broad new vistas.

We all find a level of activity that suits us. Our day is filled with eight hours of employment and eight hours of sleep, leaving one-third of the day for nonbusiness fulfillment. Some find it in front of the television screen, some with books, some with a tennis racquet or a fly rod. But there are other interests. I recommend the vibrant, exciting world of finance, a world that challenges your mind and taxes your imagination, a world that encompasses limitless opportunities for intellectual stimulation and personal profit. Many of the people interested in a mortgage investment group will have already taken steps into that world. They will help open one another's eyes.

I am not suggesting that this become a compulsion, that the members should give up bowling or bridge. I do suggest that it will add spice to their lives.

Develop a Good Habit

None of us save as much money as we could — or should. It takes more self-control than most people possess.

The popularity of Christmas Clubs and Vacation Clubs at the neighborhood savings bank testifies to that.

One of the most attractive life insurance benefits is the compulsory savings feature of the life insurance policy.

The organization form I recommend for a mortgage investment group will necessitate a monthly investment by its members. It can run anywhere from $10 a month to a hundred or more. Multiply the monthly amount you choose by twelve, compute the earnings and compound interest, continue the computation for a period of years, and you may well have your child's college education, or a portion of your retirement fund, covered — painlessly and pleasantly.

And because you will now be involved in a group, the short-sighted tendency to skip the savings just this once will be overcome. The subtle pressure of your colleagues' regular investments will keep your nose to the grindstone far more diligently than if you were alone.

Expand Your Contacts

There is no one who would not benefit from meeting more people. This cliche is true socially and intellectually as well as philosophically. It is most dramatically valid economically.

The banker, retailer, accountant, salesman, attorney, or realtor all depend upon an expanding circle of contacts to support their economic progress.

A well-planned mortgage investment group, although keyed to four professions, ideally contains a wide range of skills and experiences.

Consider architects, plumbers, and credit managers — all have an investment role to play. Electricians, furniture salesmen, and advertising men — each can contribute. People dealing in hardware, engineering — yes, even medicine — have skills to share. Discount no one. As long as the possessor of those skills is a vital person, the situation will arise where his knowledge, skill, or experience will hold the key to a problem.

It is also inevitable that the members of your investment group, of whatever background, will benefit immeasurably from being exposed to men of diverse endeavors.

A plumber? Lives there a man with piping so true who never to himself has muttered, as the escaping fluids flood his floor, "Who do I know that's a plumber?" Everyone in the group is a potential plumbing call, an insurance purchase, or an accounting client.

Group Benefits

Just as the individual members of the group will each derive personal benefits from the association, the group itself will gain from the diversity of its membership.

A group — intelligently formed and competently led — is stronger than the sum of its components.

Those strengths flow from three basic sources.

1. People lacking experience in the mortgage investment field develop the necessary skills within a short period of time. Once having acquired the skills, they add to the strength of the group by applying their own diverse backgrounds to the needs of the group. The carpeting salesman and the electrical engineer, all find circumstances where their work-a-day skills, combined with their new-found comprehension of the second mortgage investment field, provide precisely the information necessary to render the key judgment on the worthiness of a particular mortgage opportunity.

2. Your most valued source of mortgages may be the neighborhood pharmacist, or a lathe operator at the local factory. Their circle of contacts reaches many people in the course of a day, people you might never meet. After acquiring an understanding of mortgage investing, and armed with your contageous enthusiasm, they may well eliminate the need to advertise. A diverse group of participants can substantially cut the cost of mortgage investing.

3. An individual investor with $1,500 available may find an ideal borrower who needs $2,500. Magnificant though the opportunity may be, it will be lost for lack of capital. The investor may be able to raise an additional two hundred dollars, but be unable to obtain all of the necessary thousand. A group could raise the additional funds and take advantage of the opportunity.

Beware the Adventurer

It is important to set the tone early. During all your initial contacts, stress the conservative nature of your plan. Allow no one to misunderstand.

The value of early clarity becomes evident after the group is formed.

The temptation to "take a wild flyer" is in each of us, particularly when the money involved is not all our own. It's easy to sit back and decide to gamble a thousand dollars when only fifty of the thousand is yours.

If you set the tone early, and often, it will become an automatic reflex. Speculative appeals will still be made from time to time, particularly early in the game; but as they are soundly rejected each time they are proposed, they will soon cease completely.

Fie on Modesty

Do not set your sights too low. Modesty is a grievous error. Why deny the best professional appraiser in town the opportunity to participate? Invite him. You may find that he would be grateful for an opportunity to expose his skills on a continuing basis to a sizable group of the finest businessmen in town. The mortgage loan officer at the bank? Never assume he would have no interest.

Invite the best men in town.

Even if they say no, the thorough presentation of your mortgage investment plans will inevitably mean a more favorably disposed community leadership. They may recommed clients or friends. They may change their minds after you prove that your theories have practical merit.

If nothing else results from your conversation, you will have met some of the finest men in town.

7

The Structure Of An
Investment Group

Exercise Care . . . Choosing the Business Form . . . Internal Revenue Service . . . Association Criteria . . . A Sample . . . Name . . .
Introduction . . . Officers . . . President . . . Vice-President . . .
Secretary . . . Treasurers . . . Size . . . New Members . . . Invest-
ments . . . Share Purchases . . . Membership Transfers . . . Part-
ner's Death . . . Sickness . . . Disbursement Priority . . . Withdraw-
al Charges . . . Financing Retirements . . . Unpaid Shares . . .
Waiving Withdrawal Charge . . . Partial Withdrawal . . . Attend-
ance and Investments . . . Leave of Absence . . . Expulsion and
Resignation . . . Meetings . . . Voting . . . Partnership Investments
. . . Income Tax . . . Partnership Duration . . . Continuity . . .
Amendments . . . Bonding . . . Liquidating Value, Including Realty
. . . Allocating, Distributing Earnings . . . Partnership Loans . . .
Individual Endorsements . . . Additional Investments . . . Member
Loans

Exercise Care

Individual investors enjoy one enormous advantage. The money
involved is their own. They are thus able to organize their investment
procedures relatively informally, for they are responsible only to
themselves. Of course, the informality does not apply to investment
techniques, which must be assiduously followed, but rather to investment organization, which may be altered to reflect the individual's
facilities or availability.

Investment groups, however modest their beginning, soon grow to prodigious size. Informality of organization is a luxury they dare not afford, for their activities take on the dimensions of a rather sizable business within a few short years. The expansion of their activities is a reflection of the growth of their members' individual investments. Great care must be exercised to assure all concerned that the sizable individual investments are protected.

Thus, this chapter, presenting the structure of an investment group, will be minutely detailed.

Choosing the Business Form

In an effort to save hours of effort and pages of printer's ink, let me get directly to the point.

Although both the corporate and the partnership forms of business organization have unique, and appealing, benefits, I recommend that a partnership be utilized for purposes of second mortgage investment.

Creation and maintenance of a corporation involves legal fees and costs and relatively sophisticated techniques. It would insulate members from personal liability, but the personal liability risks in prudent mortgage investments are so minute there is little appeal to this corporate benefit.

A partnership gives each member a voice in management. This concept, as distinct from centralized management in the hands of the few elected corporate directors and officers, permits each member to enjoy the benefits of direct participation and the education that results.

For tax purposes, the partnership is a channel; it is not a taxpayer. It computes the income, distributes the partners' shares, and each partner then reports his own share of the partnership's profits on his own tax return.

Should the group find itself involved in the ownership of real estate, with its depreciation benefits, the partnership form would clearly permit each partner to personally enjoy the tax benefits.

Internal Revenue Service

As a result of the benefits of the partnership form, the Internal

Revenue Service has been known to examine the business structure carefully. If they determine that your "partnership" is really a corporation, following corporate procedure, they will rule it to be an association (Internal Revenue Service synonym for corporation) and will tax accordingly.

Association Criteria

Criteria for association classification are as follows:

1. Associates in a joint enterprise. Yes. Clearly, we will be precisely that. Applies to any group organized for a common purpose.

2. Seeking to transact business and share the gain. Yes. Here, again, we qualify. Doesn't any group-partnership or corporation?

3. Title to property is held by the group as a separate entity. No. Our property will be held by a trustee for the individual partners solely for convenience. Can you imagine listing seventeen, or thirty-seven, partners' names on the mortgage note and deed?

4. Centralized management. No. Except in those limited areas where the ability to move quickly is the key to success (and those areas are carefully defined, rigidly controlled, and constantly reviewed by the partners), votes of the individual partners are required for all activities.

5. Continuity of existence. Yes. The death or withdrawal of a partner does not terminate the partnership.

6. Interests transferable. No.

7. Partners enjoy limited liability. No.

The last four categories — centralized management, continuity, transferable interests, and limited liability — are the keys. We would clearly not fall within numbers 4, 6, and 7, three of the four keys. A good percentage.

I would suggest, in this changing world, that you have one of the professionals in your partnership check the format you ultimately adopt to assure yourselves of its tax status.

A Sample

Now, on to the Partnership Agreement. On the following pages I have reprinted the agreement used by an existing and successful

Connecticut investment group, Hartford Capital Fund, together with pertinent comments.

It is vital to understand that there is nothing sacred about the sample. As with all other samples, it is intended to offer an insight. If you approve, use it. If you disapprove, reword it. It is but one possible approach among many. Feel free to discard, amend, or improvise.

However you react to the following sample, I would suggest that you approach your initial group with concrete suggestions. Offer a structure, a plan.

If your modesty suggests that it might be best to offer a wide series of choices, you are mistaken. Without competent direction, it will take hours to decide upon such minor points as a name. Choose a name in advance. Propose a complete blueprint.

But never confuse positive thinking, or careful preplanning, with stubbornness.

A well coordinated approach will save much time, but your charter members, particularly if you have chosen wisely, will undoubtedly find collective solutions to some specific problem areas superior to those that you, as an individual, have been able to suggest.

Name

HARTFORD CAPITAL FUND
PARTNERSHIP AGREEMENT

Choose a name that you can wear with pride. However humble the beginnings may be, the future is unlimited. Choose one you can use after the inevitable growth and expansion.

Introduction

Recognizing the advantages of the skilled use of combined assets, the partners of this Fund do hereby join together for their mutual benefit to invest jointly certain of their funds to enable them to obtain a broad basis of investment in commercial enterprises, real estate mortgages, leases, real estate, buildings, stocks, bonds, stock rights, options, bills, notes, tax warrants, accounts receivable, chattel mortgages, conditional sales contracts, or personal property of all types, and in any other assets or enterprises of whatever type, form or description, in accordance with the following rules:

This is a purpose clause. Use it to set the target for your group's efforts. Why are they joining together? What do they plan to do? With what areas of investments will they concern themselves?

Again, don't be modest. Don't be shortsighted. You are forming a partnership for mortgage investments. Some day you may decide to use your partnership assets to purchase income producing property. There is really no limit to the investments that might intrigue your partners after they have earned their financial wings and built a sizable nest egg, a stable portfolio, and a vigorous line of credit.

Officers

1. The Fund shall have a president, vice-president, secretary, treasurer and assistant treasurer, all of whom shall be partners, elected by a majority vote of the partners at the annual meeting of the fund for one year, or until their successors are chosen.

Five officers are capable of meeting all the demands of a well organized partnership.

In the initial stages, it is possible to elect only four. An assistant treasurer is not an immediate necessity.

President

2. The president shall:
   a. Preside at all meetings.
   b. Appoint such committees as in his judgment, or in the judgment of the Fund, are advisable to the proper functioning of the Fund.
   c. Appoint an audit committee at least one month prior to the annual meeting to audit the books of the Fund.
   d. Oversee all Fund activities.
   e. Draw checks on the Fund's bank account in conjunction with the treasurer, both signatures being necessary.

The skills of the president are of vital importance. The success of the partnership is directly related to his ability to direct the activities along prudent lines, expose the membership to investment skills, transform the strangers that comprise the partnership into a cohesive unit of friends, and anticipate problems by proposing means of meeting issues before the difficulties arise.

Vice President

3.   The vice president shall assume the duties and exercise the powers of the president when he is absent or temporarily unab!e to serve; and when so acting, he shall have all the powers and be subject to all the responsibilities given to or imposed upon such president.

The vice president should be a man capable of assuming committee chairmanships. In the initial stages, many committees will be necessary to wrestle with unforeseen problems. Their reports to the partners, and recommendations for appropriate action, will do much to set the tone of the partnership. An experienced, competent vice president available for leadership within those committees will help maintain a continuity of approach, a cohesive program, and a well-integrated format.

Secretary

4.   The secretary shall:
      a. Prepare minutes of all meetings of the Fund.
      b. Preserve and bring to all meetings the Partnership Agreement and the minutes of all previous meetings of the Fund.
      c. Maintain the attendance records.
      d. Call regular and special meetings as herein prescribed.

The secretary does more than merely prepare minutes. He educates. Comprehensive reports of the previous meeting are one of the best means of providing the continuing exposure that leads to a degree of common sophistication. He assures continuity. Comprehensive minutes assure the partners that items unresolved at the last meeting will be discussed further. He provides coherence. By reference to his minutes of last fall, the membership can be reminded of the earlier solution to a similar problem. Get a good man, a thorough man.

Treasurers

5. The treasurer shall:
    a. Collect and distribute the funds of the Fund.
    b. Maintain a set of books covering the Fund's financial operations.
    c. Issue receipts to partners for their deposits when requested.
    d. Prepare monthly a statement of liquidating value as of the close of business of the last business day of the previous month for each meeting.
    e. Preserve all records and documents of a financial nature belonging to the Fund.
    f. Make all of the financial records available for inspection at all times by partners of the Fund.
    g. Prepare for the annual meeting a balance sheet, income statement, and any other necessary financial statements covering operations for the preceding calendar year.
    h. Open and maintain a bank account upon which both he and the president shall together draw checks.
6. The assistant treasurer shall perform the duties and exercise the powers of the treasurer when he is absent or temporarily unable to serve; and when so acting, he shall have all the powers and be subject to all the responsibilities hereby given to or imposed upon such treasurer.

The treasurer should be a bull-dog, a man of accounting skills, a man capable of standing in the midst of a churning stream of funds and translating them into earnings per share. If you can, find a competent Certified Public Accountant. Find another for your assistant treasurer.

Size

7. Membership shall be unlimited.

The choice of unlimited membership was made for a disarmingly simple reason: There is no way of knowing precisely how many is too much, and there is no way of knowing whether or not the ideal prospective member, embodying eagerly awaited skills, might not show an interest when the arbitrarily chosen limit has already been reached. Play it by ear. As you will see from the next section, the membership loses nothing by keeping its rolls open. It controls membership quite effectively by the exercise of voting rights. Incidentally, Hartford Capital Fund has thirty seven members and experiences no problem in achieving an effective working relationship.

New Partners

8. New partners shall be proposed at a regular Fund meeting. The election of a new partner shall be by unanimous affirmative vote of partners attending the subsequent regular Fund meeting.

Waiting until the subsequent regular meeting to vote on a proposed new member enables the partners to make inquiries and evaluate the prospect.

The caliber of partners, their skills, their reputation, their sociability, becomes increasingly important as the partnership progresses. Compatibility and ability to contribute are valid demands after the group has gotten its feet on the ground. The initial group is one you live with. Much like relatives, you learn to accept them for what they are, accommodating their idiosyncrasies and limitations. You have to, if you hope to get started.

The voting delay gives all the partners an opportunity to evaluate the prospect.

The unanimity rule assures each partner that the group will remain a comfortable one. It also suggests, though in rather extreme form, a management technique of basic importance to the partnership.

The investment group, within a relatively short period of time, will achieve an amazing financial stature. Many of the individual partners will have created a sizable stake in the success of the partnership. In such an atmosphere, bare majorities are provocative, not decisive; they alienate rather than solve. Limited majorities simply mean that a substantial number of partners disagree.

In that event, re-examine the issue. Find a solution the vast majority finds acceptable, even if it means allowing an investment opportunity to pass. Opportunities have a way of reappearing. By then, the fears embodied in a new proposal might disappear, replaced by a new-found confidence in a proposal they have had ample opportunity to analyze and with which they now have a feeling of comfort.

Growth is never a steady process. A step forward is followed by a plateau, a plateau by another tentative step forward.

Never push the group beyond its collective experience or its common sophistication.

If a proposal has sufficient merit, the group will come to recognize its validity.

If the recognition is withheld, it may well be because the proposal does not embody all the virtues claimed in its behalf.

Investments

9.   Initial membership in the Fund shall become effective upon endorsement of these Articles of Agreement, and the deposit of either $100, $200, or $300 to the Fund, which payment shall represent the purchase of four, eight, or twelve Fund shares.

10. a. Shares in the Fund will thereafter be purchased by members at $25 per share or multiples thereof, not to exceed $100 per month. Minimum investment shall be $25 per month.

The choice of investment amounts is as wide as the need and the ingenuity of your membership.

Some groups use a sizable single equal investment. Each partner might deposit five thousand dollars annually.Of course, the annual amount can vary from a modest amount to an unlimited sum. The problems created by deposits of sizable equal annual amounts are twofold:

1. A single annual payment tends to concentrate interest at that one meeting each year when moneys are deposited and the annual report is rendered. As will be discussed in greater detail when attendance requirements are analyzed, it is of vital importance that each of

the partners maintain a pattern of regular attendance. Monthly investments call for monthly attendance, as you will soon see.

2. The number of people to whom a sizable annual amount is available is quite limited. Thus, the people from whom you may choose your membership will be restricted.

I strongly recommend that the group be organized so as to permit partnership with as diverse a membership as possible.

The availability of sizable capital is no indication of the worth of a potential partner.

A sliding scale of permissible periodic investments permits the young man to participate. It also encourages the active merchant. He may not be able to maintain the same high investment each month. As business fluctuates, he has the privilege of varying his investment.

Share Purchases

10. b. Shares can be purchased only at regular meetings of the Fund by payment to the treasurer. Unless an absent partner makes his funds available to the treasurer at the meeting, his opportunity to purchase shares for that month shall lapse.

The treasurer fills a difficult position. Reports are given at every meeting and are in sufficient detail to enable each partner to follow the progress of the group.

The treasurer has books to keep, deposits to make, and checks to draw.

He should never be put in the position of pursuing partners for their monthly investments.

Investing in a competent private mortgage group is a privilege. If the member neglects to submit his monthly investment directly to the treasurer, he forfeits the privilege of investing that month. He also forfeits the money his lapsed investment might have earned.

If a partner is unable to attend, he can mail his check or ask another member to deliver it. But the check must arrive in time to be presented at the meeting. It is totally unfair to expect the treasurer to keep his books open for weeks after each session just to accommodate the languid.

Once this policy is adopted, and scrupulously followed, all late checks magically cease.

Try it.

Membership Transfers

11.   Memberships are nontransferable.

The ability to transfer memberships dilutes the individual partner's power to assure himself that the group will remain compatible.

A partner generally considers transferring his membership only when he wishes to withdraw. These recommended rules provide no means for unilateral termination other than resignation.

Partner's Death

12. a. In the event of the death of a partner, his equity, determined as of the regular meeting next following the date of his demise, shall be disbursed to his estate within six months of that determination. No penalties will be assessed. In the event commissions or costs are incurred by the Fund to secure the necessary cash, no charges will be assessed against the deceased partner's equity.

As you will note from a quick glance at Section 12d, a member resigning or expelled is subjected to a withdrawal charge as well as repayment to the group of the cost of securing the cash necessary to liquidate his account.

Obviously, the incentives to stabilize membership inherent in those regulations would be unavailing in the face of a terminal illness.

No charges, costs, or penalties are applied in the event of death.

The partnership has reserved the right to extend the payments over a six-month period, however, in an effort to protect its stability.

Sickness

12. b. In the event of the sickness of a partner, evidenced by a medical doctor's certification of the partner's inability to perform any of the duties of his occupation for a period of

ninety (90) consecutive days, his equity, determined as of the regular meeting next following the date of the medical certification, shall be disbursed within six (6) months of that determination. No penalties will be assessed. In the event commissions or cost are incurred by the Fund to secure the necessary cash, no charges will be assessed against the sick partner's equity.

A partner suffering from poor health may withdraw without charges, costs, or penalties, upon the presentation of a medical certificate.

He may also avail himself of a leave of absence without certification by a physician, under Section 14c.

Here, too, payments may be spread over a six-month period.

Disbursement Priority

12. c. The equity of deceased or sick partners, above, in that order, shall enjoy complete priority of payment of equity, with all other disbursements in payment of partner's equity suspended until death or sickness disbursements are concluded.

Payments due to a resigned or expelled partner cannot interfere with those due a deceased or sick partner. Priority is established, placing the estate of the deceased partner at the top of the list, and the medically certified partner next. Resigned or expelled partners must wait their turn.

Withdrawal Charge

12. d. Other than those categories outlined in Paragraphy 12a (death), 12b (sickness) and 14c (leave of absence), partners resigning or expelled will receive their equity, determined as of the monthly statement of that meeting at which their expulsion or withdrawal becomes effective, less any commissions, penalties, or costs incurred by the Fund to secure the necessary cash, and less a withdrawal charge. The withdrawal charge will be computed on the basis of length of membership as follows:

Through the thirty-sixth month	5%
Thirty-seventh through forty-eighth month	4 1/2%
Forty-ninth through sixtieth month	4%
Sixty-first through seventy-second month	3 1/2%
Seventy-third through eighty-fourth month	3%
Eighty-fifth through ninety-sixth month	2 1/2%
Ninety-seventh through one hundred eighth month	2%
One hundred ninth through one hundred twentieth month	1 1/2%
One hundred twenty-first month and thereafter	1%

12. e. Withdrawal shall be effective at the next regular monthly meeting following receipt of written notice by the president, or if expelled as the result of nonattendance or failure to purchase shares as outlined in Sections 14a and b, the withdrawal shall be effective as of the date of such nonattendance or failure to purchase.

Because stability is a prime requisite in the ability of an investment group to succeed, and because itinerant investors cause bookkeeping chaos, lost opportunities, and additional expense, roamers are vigorously discouraged.

This firm attitude has many benefits. People do not drop by to fill a temporary lull in their social calendars. Once accepted for membership, they respect the group and its rules. They attend meetings. They invest regularly. In short, they participate. Participation is just one step short of contribution. When the group reaches the happy state of full participation, it is just a matter of time before everyone is also contributing.

That leads to success. Full-blown success.

Nothing is more corrosive than that organization in which five officers support thirty-five members.

If your partnership is to succeed, everyone must contribute.

No-nonsense requirements will do the job.

Keep in mind that although the withdrawal charges are as high as 5 per cent, they do not result in a departing partner experiencing a loss. The earnings of any moderately competent group will always exceed 5 per cent withdrawal charges, and still leave a sizable rate of return for the former partner.

Financing Retirements

12. f.   The Fund shall not be obligated to apply more than monthly cash flow less monthly expenses to finance partner retirements, through expulsion or withdrawal.

    i. Monthly cash flow shall be defined as monthly cash receipts exclusive of borrowed funds.

    ii. Monthly expenses shall be defined as all costs, including debt service, charged to the monthly operation.

12. g.   The amount of money paid to any retiring partner shall be in proportion to the number of shares he held at the time of resignation or expulsion to all the shares of other resigning or expelled partners at the time of their resignation or expulsion.

These regulations assure the remaining partners that no sudden exodus of retiring partners will jeopardize the stability of the investment group. Only excess cash need be used, and in the event more than one partner is expelled or resigns, each retiring partner receives only his proportionate share of that excess cash.

Unpaid Shares

13. a.   Until a retiring partner's equity is fully paid, unpaid shares shall continue to share earnings.

13. b.   No monies other than borrowed funds shall be used for new investments until retiring partners in all categories are fully paid.

These sections assure current members that, in the event they choose to resign, or permit themselves to be expelled, the moneys due them will be protected. Preceding sections protect the stability of the partnership.

Used in tandem, these regulations contain a balance of protection for both the former partners and their survivors. Any competent prospective partner will look to these sections with interest.

Waiving Withdrawal Charges

13. c.   Withdrawal charges, commissions, penalties, or costs may be waived by unanimous secret written ballot of all partners

attending either the regular monthly meeting at which the withdrawal or expulsion becomes effective, or the next regular monthly meeting.

There are many circumstances lying in the gray area between the finality of death or illness and the clarity of resignation or withdrawal. A valued member of the group whose contributions have been outstanding may be compelled to resign for pressing personal reasons. A member's wife may become seriously ill, requiring funds beyond his capacity, and forcing him to reluctantly liquidate his equity.

Drafting adamant regulations permitting no deviations is unwise and unfair.

This section, though stringent, does allow the partnership to recognize deserving exceptions to the rule.

Partial Withdrawal

13. d.   A partner may not withdraw a portion of his equity.

The ability to withdraw equity at will would change the partnership from an investment group to a savings account, susceptible to the shifting tides of each member's temporary financial status.

Once again, stability is a prime requisite.

As the years pass, however, it may be necessary to establish a pattern for the systematic withdrawal of funds. Systematic is the key, for it assures stability. The decreasing withdrawal charge in section 12d and the proportionate application of excess cash in section 12f creates the basic elements of a workable framework. Workable, but not perfect.

Attendance and Investments

14. a.   If a partner shall fail to purchase Fund shares for a total of four (4) months during any twelve-month period, he shall be automatically expelled from the Fund.

14. b.   If a partner shall be absent from any three consecutive regular monthly meetings, he shall be automatically expelled from the Fund, unless adequate reason is presented,

and a unanimous written secret ballot vote of those present
is achieved.

These two sections assure the partnership of the participation of its membership. Coupled with Section 12d, they lead to an active, contributing membership.

In spite of the negative approach, these sections also lead to the establishment of a spirit of camaraderie. Many of the initial members will be strangers to each other. If, repelled by the large number of strangers attending, a member were to stay home, the strain would persist. Compulsory attendance insures a mingling that leads to fellowship.

Leave of Absence

14. c. Partners may secure a leave of absence from the Fund by 2/3 vote of Fund partners present, for a period not to exceed twelve (12) months. Unless an application for a further leave of absence is submitted and approved by the membership within that twelve (12) month period, the leave of absence shall thereupon terminate. Such partners will be considered members of the Fund only for the purposes of sharing in earnings or losses and signing evidences of indebtedness to lending institutions as the Fund may, from time to time, require.

Anticipating unavoidable absences, a partner may retain his membership by applying for a leave of absence for as long as one year. He forfeits the privilege of making monthly investments, but those funds he had invested earlier continue to share in the earnings.

Expulsion and Resignation

14. d. Upon expulsion from the Fund, a partner shall be treated as though he had submitted a written notice of resignation as of the date of said expulsion. Readmission to the Fund shall be as a new partner.

This section is a technical one, designed primarily to apply the detailed sections of the partnership agreement dealing with resigning members to those members who are expelled.

Meetings

15.   Meetings shall be held as follows:

    a. Regular meetings shall be held on the last Tuesday of each month at place determined by the partnership, unless otherwise announced at the previous monthly meeting.

    b. Special meetings may be called at any time by the president or by 25 per cent of the partners upon two days' written notice to the partners, specifying the purpose of said meeting, unless a waiver of notice signed by two-thirds of the entire membership is placed upon the minutes.

    c. The January meeting shall be the annual meeting, and the fiscal year shall be the calendar year.

Standard regulations. Obviously, you should feel completely free to vary these as widely as your circumstances dictate.

Voting

16.   Voting shall be in the following manner:

    a. Each partner, regardless of the number of shares held, shall be entitled to one vote.

    b. Voting may not be by proxy.

    c. A simple majority of the membership shall constitute a voting quorum for all meetings unless otherwise specified in this agreement.

Equal voting powers are healthy. They eliminate the cancerous resentments that inevitably arise when "the rich guys run the show" solely because they enjoy financial superiority.

Experience indicates that those who invest most tend to be known to the group. Subtly, but inevitably, their opinins are given weighted consideration. But the consideration is related to the partners' respect for whatever business acumen these men possess, not to any sense of obligation, and thus it is an infinitely healthier situation.

Proxy votes are ludicrous. No one should be permitted to isolate himself from the enlightening give and take of an open discussion, from the facts that are exposed, from the well-considered opinions that are voiced, and vote in secluded ignorance.

I prefer small quorums for social, service, or other informal organizations, but in a group that handles thousands of dollars, and compels attendance, a small quorum is both unnecessary and inadvisable.

Partnership Investments

17. Investments and loans shall be entered into or sold by a two-thirds vote of the partners of the Fund present. When purchasing second mortgages, partners of the Fund may, by two-thirds vote, delegate their authority to a committee to perform ministerial duties in their behalf in a manner specifically authorized by said Fund.

An investment group is at a marked disadvantage in a competitive investment marketplace.

First, its membership must be brought together to consider investment opportunities. Communication takes time.

Then, its partners must agree. Sometimes concurrence consumes more time than communication

In a competitive marketplace, time is of the essence. An individual investor has a great advantage.

Thus, in those limited areas where an extended repetition of experience, uniformity of partnership opinion, and continuing partnership supervision permits firm policies to be set and specific authorizations to be made, a committee can be delegated to act on behalf of the partnership.

Income Tax

18. All financial gains and losses of the Fund shall be distributable to the partners for income tax purposes, as prescribed by law.

Let me assure you that a refusal to approve this section will not eliminate the need of your partners to pay an income tax on their share of the group's earnings.

Partnership Duration

19.   The duration of this Fund is unlimited.

Using this format eliminates the need to anticipate the length of life of the partnership and eliminates those technical steps made necessary when the partners wish to continue a partnership that has exceeded its predetermined span.

Continuity

20.   This Fund shall not be terminated by the withdrawal or demise of any partner. The rights of the estate of any deceased partner shall be limited solely and exclusively to those rights set forth in Paragraph 12a.

Normally, the death or resignation of a partner dissolves a partnership. As you might imagine, dissolution creates difficulties.

At this point, you have a choice to make. Earlier in this chapter, I discussed the Internal Revenue Service criteria for associations. One, the fifth, was continuity of existence.

If you eliminate partnership termination, you encourage the Internal Revenue Service.

How's that for a dilemma?

My judgment is that the format we have been discussing is so clearly a partnership, the Internal Revenue Service would not object.

However, I make no warranties. Consult your own group's professional advisor.

Amendments

21.   This agreement may be amended by a two-thirds vote of the total membership of the Fund. A proposed amendment successfully voted upon at one meeting shall be tabled until the following meeting. Upon a second successful vote, it shall be adopted.

The second successful vote assures the partners that any amendment to the partnership agreement will not be stampeded through in a moment of passion. Again, stability is a prime requisite.

Change? Fine. A willingness and ability to change to meet new needs is necessary for the growth and success of the partnership and must be encourage. But when changes are too easy to achieve, they are too frivolously considered.

Bonding

22. The officers and employees of the Fund shall each be bonded in an amount to be determined by the partners at the annual meeting, but in no event shall the bond be less than $10,000.

Bonding is a normal, necessary, prudent business practice. It should not be overlooked. Insurance premiums are low. Any officer who objects is too naive and inexperienced to hold his position of leadership, while any employee who objects is too suspect to hold his position of trust.

Liquidating Value, Including Real Estate

23. a. Equity per share shall mean liquidating value divided by total shares outstanding.

b. Liquidating value shall mean cost of all assets, less all liabilities and expenses incurred as of the date of determination.

c. i. In the case of real estate, liquidating value shall be determined by vote of the partners after receipt of a recommendation from the Appraisal Committee.

ii. Said Appraisal Committee shall be appointed by the president with the concurrence of the partners and shall serve until replaced.

iii. Determination of value shall be made annually, whenever gross rents are increased 2 per cent or more, or whenever substantial improvements or changes are made in the physical plant or services of the property, whichever shall be sooner.

iv. The recommendation by said Appraisal Committee, as well as the vote of the partners, shall be based upon the fair market value of the property.

> v. The vote of the membership shall be binding upon all
> partners and shall stand until superseded by a sub-
> sequent Appraisal Committee recommendation and
> partnership vote.

Speaking of the willingness and ability to change to meet new
needs, the major portion of Section 23 was adopted when Hartford
Capital Fund expanded its investment portfolio beyond mortgages
and purchased its first apartment house. Nothing in the Partnership
Agreement met the special needs of real estate holdings.

Here, again, the partners exercise the authority. The Appraisal
Committee, appointed with the concurrence of the partners, merely
advises.

Tabulating the equity of the individual partners in second mortgages is relatively simple. Interest payments and decreasing mortgage
balances can be computed by a competent mathematician.

This section was designed to enable the partnership to tabulate
membership equity in the infinitely more complex area of real estate
market values.

Allocating, Distributing Earnings

> 24. a. Profits shall be allocated monthly towards Fund shares
> outstanding at the end of the preceding month.
>
> b. Profits shall be distributed at the annual meeting in the
> form of shares in the Fund. Fractional shares resulting
> from such distribution shall be applied to the recipients'
> next monthly Fund purchase.

Within these simple declaratory sentences lie the dynamics of
successful investing. Compounding earnings.

Profits are retained by the partnership for further investment.
They are distributed annually, only in the form of shares, and the
partnership retains their use.

Thus, earnings are reinvested and the partners earn interest upon
interest.

If you were to invest $100 a year at 10 per cent interest, and
withdraw the earnings each year, in ten years you would have a total of

$1,550. Had you not withdrawn the earnings, a mere annual compounding of interest would total $1,753, a 13.2 per cent greater return.

Another interesting approach is the monthly allocation of earnings. An annual distribution would simplify the duties of the treasurer, but would also lend itself to poor habits.

Under the monthly system, earnings for January are credited to those shares outstanding in December. All earnings are allocated immediately to the shares outstanding during the previous month.

There is no build-up of profits awaiting a gigantic end-of-year harvest. A pattern of regular investments is encouraged, for the partners cannot anticipate earnings bonanzas and invest sporadically to take advantage of them.

Partnership Loans

25. A minimum of three of the five members of the Executive Committee are empowered to borrow a maximum of eighty per cent (80%) of the asset value of the Fund from a lending institution, but in no event may they borrow an amount in excess of five thousand dollars ($5,000) without the approval of two-thirds (2/3) of the partners attending a meeting at which such power is authorized. The executive committee is empowered to draft a resolution to fit the requirements of any interested lending institution that, in the event of default of such notes, all Fund assets shall be used to satisfy the reasonable costs and the payment of a lending institution. The assets of the Fund shall be the security to individual partners for their personal endorsing signatures.

In order to enable the partnership to meet minor administrative financial needs as they arise, a majority of the officers are empowered to borrow a relatively small sum.

The partners, of course, retain the exclusive right to borrow sizable sums.

Because most lending institutions will require that either the evidence of indebtedness or a supplemental endorsement carry the personal signatures of the partners, the agreement assures each endorsing partner that the assets of the Fund will be applied to that debt in the event of default.

A group of twenty partners, enjoying a mortgage portfolio of $60,000, would normally be extended a loan of $30,000. If the mortgages have been chosen in accordance with the principles set forth in this book, they will be readily convertible to cash.

Thus, the individual partners need have no qualms. The debt is amply covered by convertible assets.

Individual Endorsements

26. a. Any partner, whether active or on leave of absence, given reasonable opportunity to sign a note to, or loan agreement with, a lending institution to obtain a loan approved by the partners of the Fund in accordance with Section 25, who refuses or neglects to do so, shall be deemed to have thereupon submitted a written letter of resignation to the president.

    b. Reasonable opportunity is deemed to be availability of the note or agreement at the office of the lending institution for a period of seventy-two hours after posting of written notice to the member, care of the home address last supplied by him to the secretary.

This is a minor administrative technique, designed to assure the ready availability of all members of the partnership when there is a note or loan agreement to be signed.

Once again, it is unfair to burden the group with the task of seeking out partners.

As with monthly investments, the responsibility lies with the individual partner. If he meets his responsibilities, the group functions smoothly. If he does not, the group functions smoothly after he is expelled.

Incidentally, this section also incorporates another basic philosophy of successful group management. A partnership is superior to a corporation as an investment vehicle because it exposes the partners to the problems and mechanics of day-to-day operation. It is possible for a successful group, boasting a portfolio of quality, to borrow funds upon its Executive Committee's signature. That would be a mistake, as it would insulate the partners from the dramatic education inherent in personally signing a bank note. Somehow, people are more concerned with the operations of their organization when their own signatures are on the dotted line.

Additional Investments

27. At the call of the Executive Committee, each partner shall be entitled to purchase a minimum of one share for each of the 12 preceding months during which he has been a partner, or that number of shares which will raise his total to four shares for each of the 12 preceding months during which he has been a partner, whichever number shall be greater.

This section is designed to permit the partnership to increase its ready cash in the event of need.

It is not a primary source of capital. Actually, it is an expensive way for the group to increase its investment capacity.

Funds borrowed from a bank at 6 per cent and invested at 10 per cent, add earnings of 4 per cent to the existing partnership shares.

Funds received from members of the partnership add few earnings, if any, to the existing partnership shares, for they increase the number of shares outstanding and thus spread the new earnings among more shares.

The limitations are specifically designed to help balance the financial investments of the membership. Generally, those whose financial conditions enable them to buy the maximum number of shares each month are most able to respond to the invitation. Their permissible purchases are purposely limited to enable the less committed partners to close the dollar gap.

Member Loans

28. a. At the discretion of the Executive Committee, in the sequence of requests, partners may borrow at the rate of 12 per cent per annum up to 70 per cent of their equity, which equity shall be collateral for their loan.

   b. Partner loans are a privilege, not a right. Preference is to be given third party investments when considering initiating loans to Fund partners.

c. Each borrowing partner shall sign a note, due no later than the fourth meeting of the Hartford Capital Fund following the date of said note. Due dates shall, at all times, coincide with monthly Fund meetings.

d. All partial payments of principal and renewals of partners' loans will be made at monthly meetings only.

e. Partners shall enjoy the unlimited privilege of prepayment in multiplies of $100, provided, whenever the privilege is exercised to any degree, all interest is paid to date. (A new note will then be signed for the then current balance).

f. When a partner repays his loan before the date due, interest is based upon the actual loan period.

g. When a borrowing partner becomes delinquent in the payment of his note, he will forfeit the privilege of buying new shares until the loan is fully paid. Upon being delinquent for a period of 30 days, the partner shall be treated as if he had resigned on the due date of his loan. In accordance with Article 22 of the by-laws, his equity shall be determined as of the monthly statement of said due date and shall be paid to said member less principal, interest, withdrawal penalty on the balance of said equity, and less any costs incurred by the Fund to secure the necessary cash.

h. In the event of the resignation, withdrawal, expulsion or death of a partner, the loan and interest thereon must be paid in full before the partner received his liquidating value less penalties and cost, if any.

i. No partner shall maintain a loan for a period in excess of seven months. A period of three monthly meetings shall lapse before a partner completing a loan shall become eligible to initiate a new loan.

j. A limit of 10 per cent of net Fund value shall be placed on the monies available for partner loans.

k. All requests for partner loans shall be made to the treasurer and/or the assistant treasurer.

l. When extending personal borrowing privileges to partners, the Fund may, by a two-thirds vote, delegate its authority to a committee to perform in its behalf those ministerial duties specifically authorized by said Fund.

Just as an investment group can sometimes find itself seeking additional funds in order to serve an active mortgage market, the partnership can sometimes find that its cash far exceeds its investment opportunities.

Extended periods of calm sometime descend upon the treasury. As the weeks roll into months, the temptation to grab a mortgage, any mortgage, will grow.

Ignore the urge. The temporary lull will pass. It always does — just as sure as Detroit will introduce new sports cars on easy credit terms and millions of deficit financing citizens will extend their debts further beyond their incomes to own that new sports car.

Be patient.

While you are waiting, you might find that a partner needs some short-term cash in a hurry. This section details the policies of member loans.

This section also provides a psychological safety valve.

As each partner's investment grows, a sense of concern sometimes raises its head. The money is locked in. "A partner may not withdraw a portion of his equity."

What if a personal emergency should arise? There should be a way of using that money temporarily. Section 28 is the answer. It is a conditional answer, to be sure, but it satisfies the need of the partners to feel that their investments are not totally beyond their use.

If the interest charge to partners is the same as the charge to mortgagors, the partnership will experience no loss of income should it be compelled, by exhaustion of its funds, to forego a mortgage opportunity. The borrowing partner will not suffer, either, as his own shares will participate in the profit.

Initial Mortgage Interview

Setting the Pattern

The applicant is rarely sophisticated. Oh, he's borrowed before—from the credit union at the plant or the local branch of the national personal loan company, but usually he has never taken out a second mortgage.

Your initial interview may be the key to your entire relationship. It can set the pattern for the years to come.

There are some basic attitudes you can safely anticipate:

1. The applicant is a bit embarrassed. Calling you is an admission that he needs help. Sitting before a stranger, asking for money, robs many men of their pride.

2. The applicant is suspicious. You can't blame him, really. He doesn't know you. He doesn't know if you can be trusted. Are you honest? Are your rates fair?

3. The applicant is fearful. Will you listen to his story and then laugh at him? Will you make haughty speeches about learning to live

within his income? Will you breach his confidence after he pours out his troubles?

On the other hand, the applicant may be so sophisticated that he anticipates your questions, and so calm that he seems almost unconcerned.

Whoops! Consider getting rid of him. He may know more about borrowing money than you do. And, possibly, very little about repaying.

Set a tone for the initial interview that will relieve his embarrassment, allay his suspicions, and quiet his fears. Be warm, but firm; cordial, but businesslike. Ask him who recommended him to you. Mention those who might have advised him to see you—the banker, an attorney, or a local businessman. The name dropping, if it is honest, will give him some confidence.

Better Business Bureau

Then ask whether he has called the Better Business Bureau. You will be amazed at the number who have.

This raises an interesting point. One of your first actions should be to register with the local Better Business Bureau. They will have a form for you to fill out. Do it. Then ask to see the manager. Talk to him. Tell him what you plan to do. Tell him how you plan to do it. Give him an opportunity to evaluate you.

Ask his advice. Is there anything he would like to recommend so that you can be assured you will meet the high standards of the BBB?

If your activity in second mortgage investments becomes sizable, give serious consideration to joining the local Bureau. The Bureau does a superb job for local business. It merits your support.

In any event, asking whether the applicant called the Better Business Bureau indicates your confidence in the propriety and respectability of your activities. And, certainly, being able to point to the Bureau's handsome membership placque will speak well for your business standards.

Basic Information

Back to the interview.

Ask his full name, his wife's name, his address, and his home and business telephone numbers. That's basic. How many children does he have? What ages?

What kind of home does he own? If he rents, chances are he does not own other property and will be ineligible for your mortgage loan.

How many rooms? What are they? How many baths? What kind of garage—one or two car—attached or unattached? Full basement? What built-ins—attic fan, air-conditioning, intercom system, oven, range, dishwasher, garbage disposal? What kind of heat—baseboard, hot air, radiator, oil, gas, coal, electricity? Any extras—tool shed, laundry or recreation room in the basement, cedar closet, mud room, porch? What is the size of his lot?

Sometimes pride shows through. Some people love their home, and lavish upon it the care and affection that means a clean, well-maintained property—and a determination to make prompt mortgage payments to protect the property they love.

Whatever the applicant's reaction, note it. As he thinks of your questions, his reserve melts away, exposing his qualities. Much of the worth of the loan is tied to the character of the applicant. Don't ever be so security-minded that you concern yourself solely with the value of his property.

There can be a great deal of aggravation between mortgage and foreclosure, regardless of the security of your mortgage.

There are countless homeowners who could put your money to good use. Within a short while you will meet more than your share of them.

It may not sound like a businesslike approach, but I always look for an applicant who deserves a helping hand, a man with good qualities who is temporarily hard-pressed, a homeowner who will use the mortgage money to bring stability to his family. It's a good feeling — and darned good business in the long run.

More Questions

When did he buy the house, and how much did he pay for it?

If it was more than ten years ago, the figures will not help. It might have increased in value; it might not. A recent purchase gives you a good guide. A listing of improvements since the purchase will help.

What bank holds his current mortgage? Get all the pertinent

mortgage facts: Original amount, term of years, interest rate, and current balance. The current balance is particularly important.

Also vital is the amount of his monthly mortgage payment. Be certain to ask whether the payment includes one-twelfth of his annual insurance premium, and one-twelfth of his annual real estate tax bill. If not, compute them and add them to the mortgage payment.

The next question is a waste of time: The owner's appraisal of the value of the property. Very few people are objective enough to be honest, or skilled enough to be accurate. I can only commend this question to you because it's fun. Comparing the homeowner's suggestions with the facts is a continuing source of amazement.

Now, to thicken the plot, find out how much money he hopes to borrow, and how long a period he would like to take for repayment. If he can answer both questions immediately, you can tell him how much his payments will be. Chances are, he will not make up his mind about the term of years until you tell him what the payments will be for the different terms.

Occasionally, you will meet a prospective borrower whose home does not have an equity quite large enough to meet your conservative standards. Don't give up. If everything else checks out, ask whether he has other security: A summer home with equity, or a trusting uncle who would be willing to sign his note. Many negotiations can be salvaged by additional security.

Use of the Money

Why is he borrowing the money? This is not an empty question. If he intends to use the money to build a garage, add a bedroom, or paint the house, you have a winner. This man will use your money to increase your security. If he owns a $17,000 house and borrows $1,500 to build a garage or finish the basement, the market value of the house should increase by an amount approximately equal to the size of the loan. It might not. He might over-improve the property beyond the values in his neighborhood. A modern garage done in redwood and glass might make an English Tudor uninhabitable to all but the nut who built it. But odds are in your favor.

If he intends to pay off existing loans, he may improve his cash flow position so sharply that you will have rescued an entire family.

Take typical John Applicant. He has a first mortgage, a personal loan from the XYZ Nationwide Loan Company, and an automobile loan from the Aggressive Automobile Discount Purchase Plan.

The loan company balance is $1,740, and calls for payments of $60 a month.

The purchase plan balance is $1,073.76, and carries monthly payments of $51.16.

XYZ Nationwide Loan Company	$1,740.00	60.00 monthly
Aggressive Automobile Discount Purchase Plan	$1,073.76	51.16 monthly
	$2,813.76	111.16 monthly

The balances total $2,813.76, the monthly payments equal $111.16. Applicant cannot carry those payments. He has been oversold. The pressure is impossible for him to bear. Telephone calls indicate that the loans may be paid off in full as follows:

XYZ Nationwide	$1,740.00 for $1,488.16
Aggressive Automobile	$1,073.76 for $ 907.09
	$2,813.76 for $2,395.25

A five-year second mortgage in the amount of $2,500, even at a 12 per cent annual rate, would cost $55.62 a month, or $55.54 a month less than he is now paying the loan company and the purchase plan.

The $55.54 a month that would be freed for other purposes may save his credit rating. It may mean more milk and meat on the dinner table. It will certainly release some of the pressures.

Yes, It Costs More

Obviously, the total cost to the applicant will be greater. Under the original loans, he would be paid up in two years. Now he has taken on a five-year note. It is more expensive to borrow money for a longer period of time. Chapter 4, demonstrating the marked advantage of a short-term, high-interest second mortgage as against refinancing the long-term, lower-interest rate first mortgage, is a dramatic illustration.

Add to that the fact that, because he will be making smaller monthly payments on the five-year second mortgage, there will be less money available each month to be applied to the reduction of the loan.

The total cost will be greater—greater by $518.64 to be exact. Spread out over the five years of the second mortgage, the additional money equals $8.65 a month. But—and this is the crucial "but"—he cannot afford to save the $518.64 by paying off $2,813.76 in twenty-four months. The payments are just too high. He took on more than he could handle. John Applicant and his family are choking.

Ask for a detailed itemized list of the bills he plans to pay with the proceeds.

Call the loan companies. How much will it cost to pay off an account with a $1,840 balance? The answer is often in the area of $1,490, as it is in my XYZ-Aggressive example.

Total the monthly payments. Compare the personal loan payments with your mortgage loan payments. Show the applicant the figures. Analyze them. Discuss them.

Employment, Earnings and Credit

Where does he work? What position does he hold? How long has he been with the company?

Here, again, there is much to be learned. If he has a responsible position and has been with the company for fourteen years, he is a better risk than the stock clerk who has been on the job for seven months and has been with four different companies in the past three years.

What does he earn and what is his take-home pay?

Regardless of the equity he may enjoy in his home, there is just no point in lending $4,000 at $132.86 a month to a man earning $85 a week and carrying an $84 monthly first mortgage. He will never make it. The combined payments far exceed his ability to pay.

In Chapter 9, "Investigating a Potential Mortgagor," I will discuss the Ability to Pay Formula. It will prevent you from burdening an eager applicant with payments he cannot meet, payments out of proportion to his income.

Many applicants have a second income. Ask. Some rent their extra bedroom to students, some take a second job. Many wives work. This increases their ability to pay.

Finally, get their credit information. Have they ever borrowed before? From whom, when, and how much? Where do they maintain charge accounts? Where is their checking account, their savings account?

This information, unconfirmed, will mean little to you, but it is a series of fine leads for the local credit rating bureau. Using your information as a base, the bureau will be able to provide you with a thorough report in a short period of time.

Initial Interview Form

A suggested initial interview form is shown:

INITIAL INTERVIEW

Date:

Name: Wife:
Address:
Phone — Home: Business:
Children: Number: Ages:

Style of Home: Built-ins:
   No. of Rooms: Baths: BRs:
   DR: Garage: Basement:
   Den: Heat: Extras:

When purchased: Purchase price: Lot size:
Improvements since purchase:

Bank holding mortgage:
   Original amount: Monthly payments:
   Term of years: Taxes, monthly:
   Interest rate: Insurance, monthly:
   Current balance:
Owner's appraisal for quick sale:

Other security:

Seeking how much?   For how long?   Payments:
Purpose of mortgage:
Itemize use of funds:

Ordered: Deed   Insurance policy: List of debts:

Costs cited: Legal services $
              Interest $
              Recording $

Employed:	How long:	Job:
Pay, before deductions:	Take home:	
Wife employed:	How long:	Job:
Pay, before deductions:	Take home:	

Other income:

| Other loans — from whom: | Year: | Amount: |
| Payments: | Closed: | |

Charge accounts:

Checking account:

Savings account:

Using a form is far superior to ad libbing with a blank sheet of paper. Nothing will be overlooked.

In the years to come, you will know precisely where to find the information you seek.

The applicant will have more confidence in the businesslike approach that knows precisely what questions to ask and where to put the answers.

Intuition and Documents

By now you have much of the information upon which you will ultimately base your decision.

During the interview, you will have had an opportunity to evaluate the applicant. You will know whether he is the type of man you are at ease dealing with; whether you would feel comfortable with your money in his pocket.

Your local credit rating bureau will supply more information, but keep your intuitive reaction in mind. Regardless of the credit report, lending money to a man you instinctively mistrust or dislike will add one more aggravation to your quota. Why bother? You probably have more than your share right now: traffic signals that turn red as you approach, neighbors who keep their lawns trim and lush, or a secretary who doesn't correct your spelling errors.

You will need copies of the applicant's deed to his property and the fire insurance policy on his home.

If you haven't had him bring them to the interview, ask him to mail them to you. Do nothing until they arrive. I always look to receipt of the deed and policy as an indication of the applicant's interest. Ordering a credit report, hiring an attorney, and appraising the property could involve costs and inconvenience. Do not undertake them until the applicant has taken the positive step of forwarding the papers you need.

Educate the Borrower

Take the time to spell out costs and charges in detail. To be certain that I never overlook this important detail, one section of my initial interview form contains a reminder to cite the costs of legal services, interest, and recording. It is poor business, and poorer ethics, to dangle the carrot of the money the applicant needs and blithely overlook the charges he must assume.

Applicants may be too shy, too excited, or too naive to inquire. Save him the trouble. Volunteer all the pertinent information.

Permissible interest rates are statutory. Each state varies. Chapter 11 will spell out the legal rates in detail. Local custom may vary within the legal limits.

Whatever they may be, quote them.

There are many ways of verbalizing the annual rate. Banks and loan companies rarely spell it out clearly. In our state, they offer " 6 per cent" home improvement loans. Not one-half of 1 per cent per month on the unpaid balance. No, sir. Six per cent per annum on the original loan for the life of the loan. That's about as close to 12 per cent as you can get. They sometimes add on the interest or discount the interest in advance, increasing their return.

Tell your applicants the truth.

Set them straight about the "low bank rates," too, or you will lose a good potential customer to statistical abracadabra.

I go a step further. I provide each mortgagor with a statement in duplicate at the closing. He and his wife each sign one and return it to me. I sign one for them. It sets forth the interest rates and total cost in detail. It also reprints some of the pertinent statutes regulating mortgage loans.

That form is included in Chapter 13, "Closing A Second Mortgage." It insures me that every mortgagor is aware of the financial obligations he undertakes when he signs the legal documents and accepts the loan.

Detail Closing Fees

Having assured yourself that the applicant understands the interest rate, move on to the next item: Costs.

Connecticut statutes limit mortgagees to charging for attorney's fees, including preparation of mortgage deed and note, title search, waivers, and closing fees or recording fees paid by the mortgagor.

Thus, our adjustment of costs at the mortgage closing includes only four categories.

We do not, and cannot, charge for the cost of a credit report. We do not, and cannot, charge for the cost of an appraisal. We do not, and cannot, charge for our broker's commissions.

Your attorney will know precisely what costs are permissible in your jurisdiction.

Our real estate record clerks levy a fee that varies from nine to fourteen dollars to record the mortgage deed. We estimate the probable cost and remit the balance, if any, directly to the mortgagor. Scrupulous fairness prevents us from taking advantage of the borrower. It also assures us that we have not earned one penny above the lawful earning rate.

The monthly payment includes interest for that month following the date on which the payment is due. That is, the interest is paid in advance, together with a portion of the principal. If the mortgage is closed on the fifth of a month, the first payment is often set for the first day of the following month, and that first payment will include—in advance—the interest for the days of the month that follows. Sometimes the first payment is set for one month from the date of the closing—in this example, the fifth day of the following month. Some second mortgage investors set the first payment two months ahead to give new mortgagors an opportunity to catch their breath—and to gain the opportunity to earn an extra month's interest on the full loan.

Whatever the approach, the mortgagor will be using the money from the date the mortgage closes until the date of the first payment. You are entitled to collect interest for the use of that money from the date the mortgage is signed until the first full payment is received. Approximate the advance interest payment for him during this initial interview.

We will discuss legal services in greater detail in Chapter 13, and reprint all the necessary forms. At this point, all that is needed is an indication to the mortgagor of the charge to be levied. An attorney will draft a mortgage deed and mortgage note, compute an adjustment sheet, prepare all the checks, and supervise the closing. He will provide a Certificate of Title or other title insurance. The mortgagor pays the bill.

Make it a point to question your attorney in advance so that you are in a position to advise each applicant what the fee will be.

Use of Proceeds

Advise the mortgagor that all the bills he has listed for payment from the mortgage proceeds will be paid directly to his debtors at the closing by the closing attorney. If the mortgagee prefers to use his own checks for that purpose, fine—tell him to be certain to bring his own checks to the closing, and that your attorney will mail them for him.

There's nothing to stop the mortgagor from going right back and taking out a new loan, renewing the old one, or running up the same charge accounts again—but the odds, if you have chosen wisely, are that he will be more mature. For the moment, at least, his financial affairs are in order, his credit status is good, and he can relax.

To assist in the application of the proceeds, submit two copies of this Loan Application to your prospect. (Figure 8-1)

Have him, and his wife, carefully review all their bills and list them. Then discuss which are to be paid with the mortgage money, being certain to mark those clearly. Finally, have both the husband and wife sign the form. Keep it for your file.

Prompt Payments

The last item is the most important of all, educating the mortgagor to the importance of prompt payments. Because it is of such importance, all of Chapter 15 has been devoted to it.

A word to the busy man. It is preferable, but not essential, that this initial interview be conducted in person. You can use the telephone. It

HARTFORD CAPITAL FUND
LOAN APPLICATION

Date _____

NAME _____

ADDRESS _____

This information is submitted to obtain a loan of $_____ for _____years.

We certify that the following list is a complete list of all outstanding debts, obligations, notes, mortgages, charge accounts, installment accounts, medical bills, and other monies due to creditors.

	Name of Creditor	Address of Creditor	Balance Owed	Monthly Payment (Mortgage)
1.				
2.				
3.				
4.				
5.				
6.				
7.				
8.				
9.				
10.				

The following are to be paid with loan proceeds:

NUMBERS:_____

I (We) realize that HARTFORD CAPITAL FUND will base its loan decision on the listing, and therefore certify that the above statements are true and that no existing debts have been omitted.

_____ (Husband)

_____ (Wife)

Figure 8-1.

will not be quite as effective, but you can still get your message across. The mortgage closing will give you the face-to-face opportunity to drive your message home.

To repeat, the initial interview need not be conducted in person—but it is preferable.

Investigating A
Potential Mortgagor

The Cumulative Approach

There are three major approaches to investigating a potential
mortgagor.

You cannot depend on any one of the three techniques, however
impressive your applicant seems. Nor can you depend upon satisfactory results from two investigative techniques. Unless the applicant
scores well on all three, pass on to greener pastures.

The Credit Report

The least expensive of the three, the most revealing, and the
simplest to procure, is a credit report.

Always use a professional service.

Turn to the yellow pages of your local telephone directory. "Credit
Rating and Reporting Bureaus" is the most common category. If the

choice is wide, and you are not familiar with any of the bureaus listed, call your banker, neighborhood merchant, or attorney. Any of them will be in a position to recommend a suitable bureau, based on his experience. Then call the bureau, introduce yourself, and explain your need for credit rating services. Find out what services they offer, what their charges are, what information they require, and the length of time between order and receipt.

Scheduling can be a vital issue. Some applicants must have their money in three days. If it will take you six to process their loan, they must look elsewhere.

Incidentally, if one of your applicants imposes a time limit, don't assume a superior attitude. It does not necessarily follow that an impatient mortgage applicant is a poor risk.

The initial interview form contains the basic information a credit bureau requires. Your local bureau may want additional facts: Date of birth, place of birth, or schooling. If so, add it to the form so that it becomes part of your pattern.

The charge for credit reports is generally modest. Some bureaus offer annual contracts. Discuss the fee structure in advance with the manager. Keep in mind, though, that unnecessary orders create unnecessary expenses.

Some applicants never progress beyond the initial interview. When you outline the interest rate, the costs, and your insistence on prompt payment, many prospects decide to look for someone less businesslike. And many who make that decision neglect to inform you.

That is why I never order a credit report or appraisal until I receive the applicant's deed and insurance policy. Forwarding them is akin to a commitment by the applicant. It represents genuine interest.

Sample Credit Reports

I have reprinted abstracts from two typical credit reports. They indicate the information you can expect to receive from a competent credit bureau.

Good Credit

Name: John Applicant

Address: 1655 Main Street, Hometown, Illinois

Date of Birth: 1933   Marital Status: Married

Dependents: 2 children   Character: Favorable, Normal

Ability: Subject is employed by the Wilson Widget Corporation as an engineer. He has been with them since 1-13-57. He has made consistent progress here and is now a senior technician. The firm is sound, operating on a 24-hour day schedule, and from all indications he will continue here.
Previously attended and graduated from State University. Subject also teaches a course at the local university and has done so for three semesters.

Capital: Lives at the address in a good section where he has lived for seven years. Owns this property assessed at $10,000. Personal reputation is good. Previously lived at 107 Grant Street, Hometown for one year. Previously with parents on Apricot Street, Hometown. Income is approximately $8,800 yearly, plus $1,000 per year part time work.
Savings bank reports savings account low four figures. Checking at Bank and Trust Company opened 1960, average medium three figures. Credit Union, savings low four figures.

Payments: DS Old, high $50, 30-60 days prompt.
DS Old, $90, 30-90 days prompt.
Furniture $120, paid in 90 days to terms.
Credit union, loan $1500, $100 mo. payroll deduction, bal. $800 prompt.
Men's Old, $105, revolving credit, owes current balance $55, prompt.
Women's Old, $24, 30 days, no balance.

Legal: None per our files.

Owner Information: Mortgage, Savings Bank, balance $6,998, pays $98 mo. includes escrow by 10th.

Poor Credit

Name: Henry Applicant (Mary)

Address: 199 Low Street, Hometown, Illinois

Date of Birth: 7-1-36

Marital Status: Married

Dependents: 2 children

Ability: Subject is employed at Wilson Widget Corp. as a machinist and has been with them since 10-2-64. Record is good and is offered full time work. Previously Turner Tool 3 years, record favorable. Wife employed at Wilson Widget since 2-21-65, machine work, record good.

Capital: Rents at the address in a poorer section, has lived there 4 years. Previously 144 Linden Street, Hometown. Previously 98 Little Road, Hometown, and in the local area many years. Owns no property. Income $105 per week, wife $76 per week, no other income noted. Local Trust Co. is special checking. Credit Union, savings of low 3 figures.

Payment: Tax Lien by U.S. Government, 2-13-65, $660. Credit union $697.30, 19 at $39.85, bal. $510.41 payroll deduction. Her credit union, $199.53, balance $165.90, payroll deduction. Bank and Trust Company 4-62 $195.00, paid 3-65, 7 1st, 2 2nd, 7 over 15 days, 3 over 30 days. Bank 6-66, $755.66, 12 $62 New. Auto loan 4-15-66, $640.50, 36 $17.80, bal. $314.40 Poor; Installment loan 2-65, 36 at $27.40 paid 8-66, Poor. Disc. Assoc. 4-11-64, $2,424.75, 30 $80.80, paid 4-10-64 NG. Credit Co. 2-64 $3,210.50, 36 $88.90, received one bad check.

Legal: Tax Lien U.S. Government as above.

Appraisal

An appraisal is best done by a professional — though with diligence you may train yourself to develop a degree of competence.

The simplest approach, of course, is to form an investment group that includes at least one appraiser. You may elect to reimburse the appraisers for their efforts. That is a policy decision for the group to undertake, a decision that has many repercussions. (Is the accountant paid, or the attorney?)

In any event, the well-organized investment group has a team of competent appraisers, capable of performing appraisals, and personally concerned — as investing members of the group — with the accuracy of their judgment.

An ideal situation.

The individual investor or the group that is not blessed with appraiser members, has four options:

1. Hire a professional appraiser.
2. Hire a competent realtor who has gained appraising experience.
3. If local realtors are the source of applicants, hire the recommending realtor.
4. Eventually train yourself to evaluate the property.

Hire an Appraiser

If all four options are available, look no further. Hire an appraiser. This is Mecca. An appraiser is by far the best possible initial approach.

Real estate is a gigantic industry. Billions of dollars change hands each year, based upon the value of real estate parcels and the improvements thereon. A national corporation sells a five-acre manufacturing plant. An insurance company places a mortgage on a high-rise luxury apartment complex. A real estate investment trust seeks to purchase a thriving shopping center. How are the values determined?

By local realtors? By the realtor who introduced the buyer to the seller? By the president of the corporation?

Never.

The pros use accredited appraisers, shipping them across the state lines when necessary, to assure themselves of competent skills.

There are three major groupings of professional real estate appraisers. A fourth grouping of broader professional skills, the American Society of Appraisers, combines such unrelated abilities as jewelry and automobile appraisals as well as real estate, and so will not be included.

Member, Appraisal Institute

The American Institute of Real Estate Appraisers is a branch of the National Association of Real Estate Boards.

It awards a qualified applicant the designation of Member, Appraisal Institute, commonly referred to as MAI.

To earn the respected MAI title, an applicant must be a realtor, have extensive experience in appraisal techniques, and meet many of the following requirements:

Produce demonstration appraisal reports.

Take appraisal courses at the American Institute and pass the related examinations.

Teach appraising.

Undergo a continuing character examination.

Senior Residential Appraiser

This title is conferred after successfully accumulating years of appraisal experience, collateral credits as a student and teacher, and demonstration appraisals.

SRA, as its prestigious name indicates, applies solely to residential appraisals.

As with MAI, SRA's are subject to continuing character examinations and reviews.

Senior Real Estate Appraiser

To earn the widely-respected designations of SREA, an applicant must be an active practicing appraiser skilled in appraising all forms of realty, and must make continuing contributions to the appraisal profession by teaching, writing, or providing leadership for the local appraisal chapter. An SREA must be the appraisal leader in his community. His license is granted for only a five-year period and is reviewed prior to renewal.

Will They Charge Too Much?

There they are, the elite. The leaders of their profession. Men and women who have dedicated themselves to perfecting the techniques of determining the market value of real estate: farms, shopping centers, apartment houses, and single-family residences.

Use them.

Afraid they will charge too much? Sounds logical. A professional, a man who has devoted hours upon hours of his time, and a considerable amount of money, to master the relatively obscure skills of realty appraisal, is entitled to charge more than people whose skills are less highly developed.

A cabinet-maker charges more than a carpenter, an artist more than a painter, and a physician more than a nurse.

But the remarkable fact is that the charges of a professional appraiser are very often comparable to those of the neighborhood realtor when rendering an appraisal report on a single-family residence.

By "comparable," I do not mean "exactly the same." If a local realtor volunteered to submit a report for $25.00, and an appraiser asked $35, I'd say those rates are comparable.

Often you will find realtors who charge as much as appraisers, or more. Submitting a written appraisal is not the normal pursuit of a real estate salesman. Nor is his office organized to process them. Sales data, the necessary forms, and the skilled staff, are not readily at hand. The mechanics of his office are geared to sell homes, not appraise them.

The appraiser is equipped with the necessary tools, staff, and forms. He is called upon to render hundreds of residential appraisals a year by corporate clients relocating personnel, state highway departments initiating condemnation proceedings, or local banks contemplating mortgages or foreclosures. His repeated processing of residential appraisals within the local area compels him to develop a catalogue, a staff, and a filing system that saves hours of time. He can afford to levy comparable charges, and often lower charges.

Inquire. You may be pleasantly surprised.

A Letter Report

The least expensive form of appraisal available from a professional is a simple, single page report with its accompanying certificate.

They are reproduced on the following pages.

A letter report states a conclusion. It is simple and direct. It meets our needs.

Yes, it lacks a sketch of the site, neighborhood data, legal description of the parcel, assessment information, a verbal description of the improvements, photographs of the property, details of exterior, report of interior, description of out-buildings, computations of value via cost approach and income approach, photographs and analyses of comparable sales, and a detailed summary and conclusion. This wealth of material comprises a full, formal appraisal. They are remarkable reports, encompassing a thoroughness that is a joy to behold. A thoroughness far beyond our needs.

When you interview an appraiser to determine his availability and schedule of fees, ask to see a sample of his full, formal reports. It will be an education.

JOHN ROBERTS, APPRAISER
250 State Street
Hartford, Connecticut 06103

September 8

Attorney Joseph Smith   re: Mrs. Alexander Applicant
50 Main Street   128 Tunxis Road
Hartford, Connecticut   Hometown, Connecticut

Dear Attorney Smith:

At your request, I have inspected the above-captioned property to estimate market value. It is my understanding that you are considering this real estate for security for a second mortgage.

Market value is defined as: "The highest price, estimated in terms of money which a property will bring if exposed for sale in the open market, allowing a reasonable time to find a purchaser who buys with knowledge of all the uses to which it is adapted and for which it is capable of being used.

The property consists of a single-family, 1-1/2 story frame dwelling on a lot 50′ × 150′; further described in Volume 97, page 423, of the Land Records.

I have considered all factors, including competition, location, general condition, and the market as reflected by sales of similar properties.

In my opinion, value of the above-captioned property is, as of this date:

Fourteen thousand, five hundred dollars.

Respectfully submitted,

John Roberts
MAI, SREA

JR/erh
Enclosure: Certificate

Certificate of the Appraiser

This is to certify that:

1. The facts and figures contained in this report are correct to the best of my knowledge and belief;
2. The fee for this appraisal is in no sense contingent upon the value estimate reported:
3. The undersigned appraiser has no present or contemplated future interest in the property herein appraised;
4. The opinions and conclusions herein expressed are those of the undersigned appraiser and in no way reflect those of another without due acknowledgment;
5. The undersigned appraiser personally examined the within described premises on September 7, 19 .

John Roberts, M.A.I., S.R.E.A.

Realtors

If an appraiser is not available, look to the realtors.

As in any field, there are young realtors eager to expand their skills and gain valued experience who would be pleased to work with you.

Youth is not equivalent to ignorance. They know how to find comparable sales and assessment figures. They can inspect a home and evaluate its salability.

If an eager young man, whose attitude impresses you, offers to work at a reasonable figure, use him. He will probably give you more time than his older, and busier, realtor colleagues.

On the other hand, don't underestimate the old timers. One of them may well be wise enough to see your inquiry as an opportunity to develop a mutually advantageous relationship. Appraisals can be done when the office routine slackens. It fills gaps. It also helps to fill the accounts receivable ledger, however modestly. Perhaps most important, he may be wise enough to see you as a potential client.

Inevitably, as mortgage follows mortgage, as your capital fund grows, and as your familiarity with the real estate field expands, your thoughts will flirt with outright ownership of income producing property. It is a logical step, and a predictable one.

Hiring the Recommending Realtor

If you are tempted to hire the realtor recommending a second mortgage investment, be careful. Whatever the circumstances, if the realtor is earning a commission from you for the recommendation, or if your mortgage will provide the cash necessary to conclude a sale for the realtor, he has a personal interest in gaining your approval.

That conflict of interest is difficult to overcome.

It would be best not to put yourself in that position until you are knowledgeable enough to ask the right questions and experienced enough to evaluate the answers.

Train Yourself to Appraise

This should be your ultimate goal. It will take time, patience, and a willingness to learn — but it can be done.

There are some superb instructional books, books that detail appraisal techniques. Try your local library. When you find the right one, read it. Buy it. Make marginal notes. Abstract it. Reread it.

Nothing is quite as exciting as finding a book that carries the information you need.

Your appraiser may be willing to have you accompany him when he sets out to evaluate your applicant's property. This is a question that you might consider asking him before he is hired. He may enjoy the idea of having you witness his skills. Be an appreciative audience and an observant one. Ask only a few questions — but make them count.

If you have taken the trouble to find and read a good appraisal book, many of his techniques will be apparent to you. You will also be able to speak his language and use the terms that are common to his work. Generally, that opens the door. Here's someone he can talk to. Here's someone who understands. You may well find that your few questions are replaced by his flow of comments.

Drink it all in. It's pure gold.

As appraisal follows appraisal, you will learn how to find comparable sales and evaluate them, how to locate tax information and use it.

The local market will lose its mystery. You will come to know the different sections of town, the preferable locations, the trouble spots.

Your reading habits will change. You will find the classified ad section one of the most intriguing portions of your local newspaper. Glancing at it with some regularity will give you an education in depth.

As you become familiar with the geography of your area, an advertisement for a "seven room cape cod with two car oversized garage, flagstone patio, enclosed porch, fenced in yard" for $23,500, on Rogers Street, will create a picture in your mind, a picture that will be a reference point for the future.

You might find yourself in that section of town the next day. Look at the advertised home. Why has the owner valued it at $23,500? Is he realistic?

At first you will not know. Real estate values are comparative. One house is worth two thousand dollars more than another house because it offers something more than the other: location, size of lot, number of rooms, etc.

As your fund of information grows, you will soon find that the six-room ranch in the south end of town is exactly the same as the one that sold for $17,000 last month. Location? Same general area. Condition? The trim needs painting, but the effect is minor. After thinking it out, you realize that there is only one basic difference — last month's $17,000 home did not have a garage. This one does.

Suddenly, the problem becomes a simple one. You are no longer evaluating a six-room ranch. Merely a one-car garage, unattached. This is the key to real estate valuation. Comparable sales. Know them and you know the market.

I am not suggesting that by next Thursday you will be able to open a real estate appraisal office.

I do suggest that by reading professional texts, hiring and observing a professional appraiser or competent realtor, following newspaper reports of houses for sale or sold, and personally inspecting a large number of residences, you will develop a skill of sufficient degree to fall within 10 to 15 per cent of true market value.

Other Clues

What valuation did the town assessor use in determining the assessment for tax purposes? The assessed value is available for the cost of a telephone call. If your town assesses at 65 per cent of value, or 50 per cent, the assessor's valuation is just a mathematical computation away.

You might make it a point to visit the assessor personally, instead of using the telephone. The dime saved won't mean much, but the personal relationship could mean a great deal.

After a few visits and a number of inquiries have established some rapport, you might logically ask why this cape on Ann Street is carried at $16,700, when the cape on Irving Avenue was listed at only $15,300.

If the telephone doesn't interrupt, and if the office activity is slow, you just might have found yourself another teacher.

People are naturally friendly. People are also naturally gregarious. And nothing warms a heart faster than someone who is interested in you, your job, and your thoughts. If you can project a natural friendliness and a sincere interest in his work, the assessor may find your questions hard to resist. But keep in mind that I did not refer to the assessor's valuation as the answer — only a clue. It is not conclusive and it may be misleading.

What valuation did the bank put on the property? This is not a simple question to answer. But you do have some indications. By checking the land records you can determine the mortgage amount, interest rate, and term of years. If your local mortgage market is constant, and if the bank that wrote the mortgage charges a 6 per cent annual interest, for 80 per cent, 25-year mortgages, you have the means to approximate their valuation.

This approach is far from foolproof. The best that can be said about it is that if you have already found a value and are looking for a confirmation, the mortgage analysis approach may help. Don't ever rely upon it.

The United States Government directs that documentary stamps be affixed to every deed reflecting the sales price to the extent of $.55 per five hundred dollars or part thereof.

If you check the land records in your community's recording office and find a notation of $18.70 in documentary stamps affixed to the deed, the sales price was probably somewhere between $16,500 and $16,999.

Probably. There is no law against adding a few dollars' worth of stamps to a deed. Some investors do it as a matter of course. Fortunately, few purchasers of single-family dwellings bother.

If the property was purchased subject to the seller's mortgage, that is, if the buyer has assumed and agreed to pay the seller's mortgage instead of getting his own, the documentary stamps will sometimes reflect the difference between the selling price of the house and the balance of the mortgage the buyer has assumed. In those cases, the deed will usually specify the mortgage balance, so it's a simple matter of arithmetic: Mortgage balance plus documentary stamps equal sales price.

If the house costs $18,000 and the buyer assumes and agrees to continue paying the seller's mortgage, which the deed reports has a balance of $13,000, the United States documentary stamps will then generally equal $5.50.

Documentary stamps are a relatively accurate indication of sales price — and if the sale was a recent one, they will provide a fine clue to market value.

Title Report

A man with an acceptable credit report and an amply-valued house might still not pass our inspection. He might own the home jointly with his wife, father, or aunt, and be unwilling to have his co-owner know that he is borrowing money. He might have a sewer caveat, a tax lien, or an attachment against the property, severely limiting his equity. Any one of countless fact situations might eliminate him as a mortgage candidate.

Only an examination of the land records can uncover those problems.

Call your attorney. He will provide a detailed report and specific recommendations.

He might tell you that the mortgage deed and note must be signed by both John Doe and his sister, Mary Smith. He might report that there is an old mortgage on record which seems to have been paid in full, but that it will be necessary to record a release of that aged mortgage before proceeding with your mortgage.

Follow his advice.

If all three investigations result in good news, you are ready to proceed with the mortgage.

10

The Ability-To-Pay And
Safety Formulas

Evaluating Your Security ... Ability-To-Pay Formula ...
Take-Home Pay ... Taxes and Insurance ... A Second Income
... Wife's Employment ... Other Variables ... Applying the
Ability-To-Pay Formula ... Safety Formula ... Existing Mort-
gage Balance ... Amount of Second Mortgage ... Property Ap-
praisal ... Computing the Safety Formula ... Either or Both?

Evaluating Your Security

All of the techniques outlined thus far mean nothing, absolutely
nothing, if your investments are speculative.

The finest organization methods, the most astute appraisals, the
most penetrating credit analyses, the most competent title examinations and the most inspiring initial interviews are all a waste of time
unless you have a means for evaluating how prudent, how secure, and
how conservative your prospective mortgage will be.

Let's assume that the owner of a $16,000 home, carrying a $14,000
mortgage, wants a $1,500 second mortgage. His credit report is fine.
His title is flawless. He said all the right things at the interview.
Should you lend him the money?

No. His Safety Formula registers 96.8 per cent.

The decision is not an emotional one. Basically, a successful
mortgage investor is a mathematician. He uses two simple, but won-

drous, mathematical formulas. Armed with these, he walks to the very mouth of the dragon's lair and emerges unscathed.

Intuition, or evaluation of the applicant's attitude, comes into play only after he passes the formidable barriers of both of these tests.

Each formula is based on an elementary principle, the foundation of our investment philosophy:

Second mortgage financing should be a conservative investment.

There are two basic questions to be answered:

1. Is the mortgagor capable of meeting the mortgage payments?
2. In the event the payments are not made, is the property capable of protecting the money you have invested?

Ability-to-Pay Formula

When the United States government entered into the mortgage insurance field, via FHA and VA mortgages, it established a simple rule of thumb for gauging the capacity of prospective mortgagors to meet their mortgage payments.

The theory was, and still is, that monthly fixed expenses (mortgage payments, auto loans) should not exceed one quarter of the month's take-home pay.

Take-Home Pay

Take-home pay is the weekly salary less income tax deductions, union dues, withholdings, pension contributions, etc. — whatever the worker finds in his envelope after each salary period.

Because we often use our second mortgage money to pay off the mortgagor's existing loans, his fixed monthly expenses are invariable limited to the monthly payments on his first mortgage and his prospective second mortgage.

Thus a man carrying a first mortgage with monthly payments of $107, and seeking a second mortgage that would call for monthly payments of $33.37, should have a weekly take-home pay of $140.

Taxes and Insurance

Now, it is not quite that simple. In computing the first mortgage payments, an amount equal to both one-twelfth of the annual real estate taxes and one-twelfth of the annual fire insurance premium should be included.

Often they are. A $12,000, 6 per cent twenty-five year mortgage carries equal monthly amortization payments of $77.32. That is, after 300 monthly payments of $77.32, the mortgage would be fully amortized, or paid. Many banks create an escrow account and add to that monthly payment of principal and interest an amount that will enable the bank to pay the tax and insurance bills in full, directly from the escrow account. Their reasoning, incidentally, is that their basic security lies in the real estate. A fire, or a tax sale, could wipe out their security. By paying both the insurance premium and the tax bill directly, the mortgagee eliminates the fear of loss as the result of fire or tax delinquency.

If taxes are $300 per year, an additional $25 will be added to the $77.32 each month. If the annual insurance premium is $60, an additional $5 will be included. The total then becomes $107.32.

If your applicant's monthly mortgage payments do not include taxes and insurance, compute them and use the total figure in applying the Ability-to-Pay Formula.

A Second Income

If the applicant holds two jobs, you can use both incomes only under certain circumstances.

Exercise judgment.

The supplemental income of a filing clerk who took on an evening job stoking coal at the local plant three weeks ago should not be included.

Why?

The odds are that our filing clerk will not be equipped to hold the job. The skills are too dissimilar. Further, he has held his second job for such a short period of time we have no basis upon which to assume that stoking coal is anything but a temporary gesture.

Look to two criteria: ability to meet the demands of the second job, and history of successfully adjusting to the rigors of holding a second job.

An English teacher who, for the past ten years, has earned a supplemental income acting as local reporter for the big city newspaper deserves to have both incomes combined in determining his ability to pay.

Wife's Employment

In some cases, the applicant is married and his wife is employed.

Here, again you should not automatically combine the net incomes. There are many criteria to be considered.

If she is a nurse, a teacher, or a professional in any other area, has a history of steady employment, and has mature children, by all means, add her take-home pay to her husband's.

A wife's income should be analyzed in the same manner as her husband's: ability and history. But, bless them, women create special problems. For one, they are susceptible to pregnancies, and a new-born babe is incompatible with the schedule of all but the hardiest working mothers. For another, if they are blessed with a large family of young children, there are bound to be many hours of lost time to cover the mumps, chicken pox, and unexpectedly unavailable baby sitters.

Once again, exercise judgment.

All factors considered, if you feel she has less than a fifty-fifty chance of maintaining an income for the life of your second mortgage, do not use her take-home pay in applying the Ability-to-Pay Formula.

If the odds of continued employment are higher, consider utilizing a portion of her take-home pay in the Formula.

Always keep in mind, when evaluating second incomes, that we are not talking of the distant future. Our concern is basically limited by the term of mortgage the applicant is seeking.

Other Variables

Other variables exist. Some men declare less than the number of dependants to which they are entitled for income-tax purposes. As a result, more taxes than necessary are withheld from each pay check. As a further result, when the moment of truth arrives, and the income tax return is filed, these cunning plotters often earn sizable refunds.

If your applicant follows this pattern, and his current withholding pattern is similar, his net income should be increased for Formula purposes by a weekly sum proportionate to the annual refund. He can always change the pattern to increase his weekly take-home pay.

Does his employer allow him an automobile for his personal, as well as business, use? Is gas, oil, insurance, or maintenance included? Whatever the benefits may be, they are truly income in today's auto-owning economy. It is safe to assume that if the business automobile were not available, applicant would be using some of his income to buy and maintain a replacement.

Add a reasonable amount to applicant's take-home pay.

Is applicant blessed with an expense account? If he is merely reimbursed for actual expenses, his income would not benefit directly. No problem. But if the account were a lump sum and beyond his actual needs, he would clearly be entitled to have the expense surplus calculated on an average weekly basis and added to his take-home pay.

There are many other similar fact situations calling for independent judgment. Be conservative. Be realistic. And be cautious.

Must the figures be in perfect balance? No. An applicant boasting a continuing history of steady employment need not hit the weekly income on the nose. If he earns $140 and needs $147, consider the Formula in balance. A 5 per cent variance is permissible in appropriate circumstances.

Applying the Ability-to-Pay Formula

The Ability-to-Pay Formula is simple in the abstract. True, there are circumstances where you must exercise discretion, but those situations are solved by a dose of old-fashioned common sense.

The Formula becomes more difficult to apply when you interview an applicant face-to-face.

He's an easy-going fellow — soft spoken. His finger nails tell you he is a hard worker. His wife's been ill. He had to hire a girl to watch the kids, five of them. The wife's better now, but the bills piled up. He has three loans costing a total of $178 a month. His mortgage, including taxes and insurance, costs $133 a month. His take-home pay is $140 a week. He's looking for a part-time job and so is his wife. The loan payments are just too much for him to carry. Oh, he hasn't fallen behind, but in order to pay the mortgage and the loans, he has accumulated a sizable milk bill, an impressive grocery bill, and owes the doctor quite a bit.

He could pay the three loans in full, the dairy, food and medical bills, with a second mortgage that would cost him only $88.98 a month.

He reminds you that he is paying $178 every month now for the three loans. If he can do that, he certainly can manage to pay you half as much each month.

What do you do? He's right across the desk from you. He needs help. And he's obviously a nice guy. You like him.

It is not easy, but if you want to help him — do not extend him a mortgage loan.

Forget about your financial exposure. Think of the applicant. What is the benefit to him of a five-year loan he cannot repay? His two mortgages would cost a total of $230 a month. He takes home $140 a week. He may be better off for a few months, perhaps a year. But inevitably, inexorably, the pressure will wear him down. He will start falling behind in his payments. One sickness. A temporary lay-off.

You do not help a man by lending him more than experience indicates he can afford to pay.

As for you, if you find it difficult now to refuse this likable applicant, and his five children, how will you feel in a year or so when the pressure of a loan you should never have granted puts the mortgage in default? How will you feel starting foreclosure proceedings to protect your investment?

Safety Formula

If the Ability-to-Pay Formula is valuable, the Safety Formula is the very heart of successful mortgage investment.

A judgment error in applying the Ability-to-Pay Formula or a misread credit report can each cause problems, but whatever mistake has been made can be rendered relatively harmless to the investor's ultimate security if the Safety Formula has been scrupulously followed.

The Safety Formula transforms a gamble into an investment. Understand it, and apply it, and you will elevate your portfolio into a conservative investment that earns a high rate of return, opens lines of credit, and is available for immediate liquidation.

The Safety Formula is composed of but three figures:

1. The balance of the existing mortgage.
2. The amount of the second mortgage the applicant is seeking.
3. A realistic appraisal of the property.

Let's pause for a moment and consider each of the categories.

Existing Mortgage Balance

Ask the applicant for his mortgage balance. His answer will rarely be close enough to the facts to enable you to make an accurate application of the Formula, but he will give you an approximate figure.

"Twelve thousand dollars." More often than not, that means his balance is $12,897.14.

"Around thirteen five." The balance could be anything up to $16,000.

Generally, the applicant underestimates by anywhere from $1,000 to 10 per cent, whichever is greater.

Note his estimate on your Interview Sheet. There's no point in going any further until you see how the other Safety Formula figures compare.

If the other figures indicate that the applicant has some potential, there are three sources for an accurate mortgage balance:

> (a) The current monthly mortgage payment slip. It generally contains a great deal of information: amount of monthly payment, portion of the payment to be applied to interest, portion to be applied to reduce the principle, tax and insurance escrow payment, as well as mortgage balance. The mortgage balance amount, incidentally, is generally the balance prior to the current payment. If the current payment has already been made, deduct the portion applied to principal from the last mortgage balance cited.

> (b) The credit report. If the applicant has potential, you will be ordering a credit report after receiving his deed and insurance policy. The credit bureau will include his mortgage balance in their report.

(c) The bank. A business-like call to the mortgage department of the bank holding applicant's mortgage will generally unearth the principle balance.

Amount of Second Mortgage

Obviously, you are the primary source of the amount of the second
mortgage the applicant is seeking. Yet even here you have some
discretion. Applicant asks for $2,200. After analysis, you discover his
circumstances are such that $1,700 would be sufficient.

Use the lower figure. The more applicant borrows, the higher his
monthly payment will be. The more applicant borrows, the longer
period of time he must generally take to repay the loan. Either
circumstance costs him more money.

My concern is not solely for the applicant. Keep in mind that the
lower the cost and the shorter the payments, the less opportunity for
trouble.

Never allow the excitement of a long-term loan, with correspond-
ing low monthly payments, to stampede an eager borrower into going
in over his head. By lending a $2,200 applicant only the $1,700 he
needs, you can cut his monthly payment by approximately $15, or
shorten his mortgage from a five-year note to a three-year note. Either
approach benefits both of you.

One further point. It is to your advantage to keep your mortgages
small. The smaller the better. In this way, should you err, the impact is
minimized. One $4,500 mortgage certainly exposes you to a greater
potential loss than one of three $1,500 mortgages.

Property Appraisal

The appraisal of the property is the most elusive of the three
figures comprising the Safety Formula.

We discussed the sources of appraisals in Chapter 9. Having
chosen your appraiser, what do you ask him to find? Replacement
cost? No. We couldn't care less what it would cost to replace the
applicant's house. Fair market value? Close, but fair market value
does not really meet our special needs.

If the time should ever arise when it becomes necessary to
safeguard your investment by compelling a foreclosure sale, you

would not realize the fair market value. An enforced sale under the gun may bring a lower price. Someone trying to unload quickly often accepts less than the man who can sit for a while.

A strict foreclosure would be worse. There, add court costs, attorney's services, and committee's fees to the lower sales price.

The point is, you are looking for the "unloading" price, the price at which the property will sell within one week. If you are using a realtor, you might describe what you seek as the price at which he would be pleased to accept a one-week exclusive listing for the sale of the house.

When you have the quick sale price of the house, the mortgage balance and the amount of the second mortgage, you are ready to apply the formula.

Computing the Safety Formula

$$\text{SF:} \frac{F + S}{QSP}$$

The Safety Formula is the first mortgage balance plus the new second mortgage, divided by the quick sale price of the property.

F = first mortgage balance

S = second mortgage balance

QSP = quick sale price

$$\frac{\$12,417 + \$1,500}{\$16,500} = \frac{\$13,917}{\$16,500} = $$

.843 or 84.3%

$$16,500 \overline{)13,917.000}$$
$$13,200\ 0$$
$$\overline{\quad 717\ 00}$$
$$\quad 660\ 00$$
$$\overline{\quad\quad 57\ 000}$$
$$\quad\quad 49\ 500$$

The final portion of the Safety Formula is the margin for error, the difference between the mortgage totals and the quick sale price.

In our example, the margin for error is $2,583. That is, should the home produce net proceeds of $2,500 less than your appraised value, your investment would still be secure.

The complete Safety Formula for our example would read as follows:

84 per cent + $2,583.

The Safety Formula, applied to the mortgages held by Hartford Capital Fund shows an approximate 65 per cent + $8,000 average, year after year. That is an almost impregnable investment situation.

Do not be misled by the 80 per cent mortgages so freely offered by banks. Some banks offer mortgages as high as 90 per cent.

If your mortgages are to have the safety, the comfort, and the ease of truly conservative investments, keep a 70 per cent average for your portfolio. One 95 per cent mortgage and one 45 per cent mortgage average 70 per cent. Obviously, I do not advocate that. A 75 per cent and a 65 per cent, yes.

Steer clear of anything above 80 per cent. I know that there are mortgage investors in your community who readily offer 90 per cent loans. There are automobile drivers who knowingly drive on bald tires.

Don't for a moment believe that the only potential mortgagors are border-line risks. That's just not so. There are many, many fine homeowners waiting to be served.

They are not as numerous. They are more difficult to find. But, they are worth the patience and the effort.

And, as Chapters 18 and 20 will graphically show, a conservative mortgage average will open the door to two astonishing benefits that will sharply increase your earning capacity and measurably increase your peace of mind.

Either or Both?

This chapter, dealing with mathematical standards for evaluating the investment quality of prospective mortgagors and mortgages, is incomplete without one firm, final admonition.

The applicant must pass both tests, not just one. And he must pass each of them decisively.

A borderline ability to meet your monthly payment schedule inevitably means problems somewhere along the line. Whether it be sickness in the family, extensive automobile repairs, a strike at the plant, or a new set of golf clubs, something will happen to upset the carefully balanced flow of funds during the life of your mortgage. Life always holds surprises. And pregnancies. And storm damage. And dental emergencies. You must be protected by the margin for error built into the Ability-to-Pay Formula.

Yes, a solid Safety Formula will ultimately protect your investment, but a superb Safety Formula does not eliminate the aggravation of policing late payments or pursuing checks drawn on insufficient funds.

Yes, a solid Safety Formula will ultimately mean a successful foreclosure, but you are not investing in mortgages in order to play the villain. Nor to own foreclosed real estate. All you are interested in is endorsing checks to your account.

You have confidence in your appraiser. He's a pro. But you would prefer not having to test his skill in the harsh realities of the auction market.

If the Ability-to-Pay Formula prophesies trouble, and you proceed in spite of the cold mathematical warning, your reward will be hours of effort, aggravation, and concern.

The same attitude must govern your use of the Safety Formula. Insist that both show satisfactory results.

11

Legal Restrictions

Usury ... Racketeering ... Respectability ... Follow the Spirit of the Law ... Limitations of the Charts ... Your Attorney ... The Legislature Speaks ... Legal Rate of Interest ... Maximum Interest Rates ... Are Corporations Excluded? ... Recognizing Realities ... One View ... The Need for Writing ... The Penalties for Usury

Usury

This is the area with which you must gain complete familiarity. It involves a most serious problem for second mortgage investors. Usury. This is the area within which unscrupulous persons have taken advantage of hard-pressed homeowners. This is the area that prompted warnings by the National Better Business Bureau, a lengthy inquiry by the New Jersey Real Estate Commission, and grand jury investigations in Ohio and Indiana.

Usury is the taking of a profit on a loan greater than the lawful rate of interest. There are a number of unprincipled loan sharks who follow this pattern. Unable to appeal to the courts to help collect these usurious, and illegal, debts, they resort to threats and violence. Witnesses before the New York State Investigation Commission told of shots fired into their homes, bombs exploding in their cars, and telephone death threats.

The loan sharks operate primarily in the unsecured loan areas, however, not in the second mortgage field.

Racketeering

There are second mortgage racketeers, however, enough of them to create a serious public relations problem for the substantial firms and honorable individuals engaged in legitimate second mortgage investments.

The National Better Business Bureau reports that an Ohio woman, who borrowed $3,000, found herself obligated to repay $97.50 a month for sixty months, for a total of $5,850.

The interest rate was legal, but her charges were:

Title Search	$35.00
Credit Report	20.00
Investigation Cost	30.00
Preparation of Instruments	50.00
Placement Fee	1,375.00
Brokerage Fee	450.00
Recording	20.00
Appraisal	45.00
Closing Costs	50.00
	$2,075.00

The *New York Times* tells of a New Jersey borrower seeking $4,800 who became indebted for $9,600, including a placement fee of $3,900, 6 per cent interest on the face amount of the five-year loan, and other charges.

These sad and infuriating tales are endless. Jackals are feeding on the bones of homeowners in every state in the nation.

Their existence will make your investment career thornier than it need be. Some prospects may tend to equate you with the immoral minority. The vast majority, however, will recognize you for what you are and welcome your assistance.

Respectability

There are many steps on the road to respectability. I discussed joining and working with your local Better Business Bureau in Chapter 8.

Applying the Ability-to-Pay Formula, discussed in detail in Chapter 10, will prevent you from permitting a potential borrower to become an overburdened debtor.

Utilizing the forms reproduced in Chapter 8, particularly the Statement of Loan form, and following the procedures recommended, will assure you that your borrowers will be fully aware of all their obligations—item-by-item, and in the aggregate.

Scrupulously examining your state statutes, and rigidly adhering to the letter and spirit of their limitations, will keep you well within honorable bounds.

Follow the Spirit of the Law

The key here is not the letter of the law, but the spirit.

Your intention is to lend money, on a secured basis, to sincere citizens temporarily hampered by lack of cash and/or credit. You seek a reasonable return. You will not take advantage of anyone. You will prevent an eager debtor from borrowing more money than he can afford to repay. You will make certain that every portion of the transaction is fully understood. You will be certain that the funds are used for the purposes lent. Having received prompt and full payment, you will do all that you reasonably can to improve the borrower's credit rating by informing inquiring credit agencies of his high degree of responsibility.

Yes, you are there to make a profit. But only a legal one. Only a clean one.

Unfortunately, homeowners unaccustomed to the unrelenting pressures of creditors can become panic-stricken when facing a debt situation. In situations of this sort, the letter of the law is not always a sufficient guide. Apply the spirit, too. That is, unless you have found a way to shave without looking yourself in the eye every morning.

Limitations of the Charts

On the following pages, I will set forth five key statutory provisions for every state in the nation as well as the District of Columbia, Puerto Rico, and the Virgin Islands.

The charts will give you some insight into the limits you must observe.

Let me be perfectly frank and meticulously candid, however. These charts are neither complete nor up-to-date. They cannot be. Limitations of space do not permit a discussion of all the diverse factors that apply in the second mortgage area. Such relevant considerations as late charges, permissible closing charges, interest rate after default, site for recording mortgage instruments, and local recording charges, have not been tabulated.

Limitations of skill do not permit one man, however well trained or determined, to accurately and concisely analyze and summarize fifty-three series of statutes and their interpretations, fifty-two of which are foreign to his experience. Interpretations of statutes are vigorously contested in every court in the land. The accuracy of any interpretation is not known until the highest court in the state has spoken. Sometimes not even then.

Limitations of the passage of time do not permit the inclusion of changes in the law as legislatures amend existing statutes. The amendment process is constant and pervasive.

All of which means that you are to view the five charts solely as a general guide. To follow them without further assistance is to proceed at your peril.

Your Attorney

Is there anyone astute enough, blessed with the requisite experience in the laws of your state, and capable of keeping himself abreast of all the amendments applicable to your law?

Of course. Your attorney.

No one, not even your brother-in-law, the one who can quote Babe Ruth's 1927 batting average, is wise enough to plunge ahead without a guiding hand.

Let me assure you, should the thought cross your mind, that your attorney—or if you have not yet dealt with one, any competent attorney you choose—will welcome your mortgage inquiries. Don't apologize, even if your start is a modest one. My example in Chapter 1, based on minimum figures, produced eight mortgage closings for an attorney in five short years.

The Legislature Speaks

The regulations controlling the amount of interest that may be charged under any agreement for a loan of money are found exclusively in the statutes of the individual states. They are legislative, not judicial. That is, the interest laws are made by the legislators of each state. Courts of law enforce and interpret the statutes, but do not determine the permissible percentages or, generally, the manner of application.

Legal Rate of Interest

The most prevalent interest rate, least known to the layman, is usually referred to as the legal rate of interest. It is the interest rate applied to a loan when the parties to that loan have not specified a rate of interest.

One such statute is Section 37-1 of the Connecticut General Statutes, which reads:

"The compensation for forbearance of property loaned at a fixed valuation, or for money, shall, in the absence of any agreement to the contrary, be at the rate of 6 per cent a year; and in computing interest, three hundred and sixty days may be considered to be a year."

In other words, a note by means of which John Doe borrows $500 from Richard Roe is interpreted to read "$500 at 6 per cent interest per year," unless the note either specifies a particular rate of interest or states that no interest will be charged.

Legal rates for the fifty states, the District of Columbia, Puerto Rico, and the Virgin Islands, follow.

LEGAL INTEREST RATES

Alabama	6%	Alabama Code, 1958, Title 9, Section 60
Alaska	6%	Alaska Statutes, 1962, 45.45.010
Arizona	6%	Arizona Revised Statutes, 1956, Section 44-1201
Arkansas	6%	Arkansas Constitution, Article 19, Section 13
California	7%	California Constitution, Article XX, Section 22
Colorado	6%	Colorado Revised Statutes, 1963, Chapter 73, article 1, Section 1
Connecticut	6%	Connecticut General Statutes, 1958, Section 37-1
Delaware	6%	Delaware Code, Title 6, Section 2301

LEGAL INTEREST RATES (Continued)

D.C.	6%	Code of the District of Columbia, 1961, Section 28-3302
Florida	6%	Florida Statutes, 1965, Section 687.01-02
Georgia	7%	Code of Georgia Annotated, Section 57-101
Hawaii	6%	Revised Laws of Hawaii, 1955, Chapter 191
Idaho	6%	Idaho Code, 1947, Section 27-1904
Illinois	5%	Illinois Revised Statutes, 1965, Chapter 74, Paragraph 1
Indiana	6%	Burns' Indiana Statutes Annotated of 1933, Title 19, Chapter 20, Section 1
Iowa	5%	Code of Iowa, 1962, Chapter 535, Section 2, as amended in 1963, Chapter 317, Section 1
Kansas	6%	Kansas Statutes Annotated, 1965, Chapter 16, Article 20
Kentucky	6%	Kentucky Revised Statutes, Official Edition 1964, 360.010
Louisiana	5%	Civil Code Revision of 1870, Article 2924
Maine	6%	Maine Revised Statutes Annotated, 1964, Title 9, Section 228
Maryland	6%	Michie's Code 1957 Edition, Article 49, Section 1
Massachusetts	6%	Massachusetts General Laws, Tercentenary Edition, 1932, Chapter 107, Section 3
Michigan	5%	Compiled Laws of 1948 & Mason's 1961 Supplement thereto, Section 438.51
Minnesota	6%	Minnesota Statutes, 1961, Chapter 334, Section 1
Mississippi	6%	Mississippi Code of 1942
Missouri	6%	Missouri Revised Statutes, 1959, Section 408.020
Montana	6%	Revised Codes of Montana, 1947, Title 47, Chapter 12, Section 4
Nebraska	6%	Revised Statutes of Nebraska, 1943, Section 45-102
Nevada	7%	Nevada Revised Statutes, Section 99.040
New Hampshire	6%	New Hampshire Revised Statutes Annotated, 1955, Chapter 336, Section 1
New Jersey	6%	Statutes Annotated, Section 31:1-1
New Mexico	6%	New Mexico Statutes Annotated, 1953, Chapter 50, Section 6-16

LEGAL INTEREST RATES (Continued)

New York   6% Consolidated laws of 1909, General
                       Obligation Law Section 5-501(1)
North Carolina 6% General Statutes of North Carolina,
                       Chapter 21, Section 1
North Dakota   4% North Dakota, Century Code Annotated
                       Section 47-14-05
Ohio   6% Baldwin's Ohio Revised Code Annotated,
                       1953, Chapter 13, Title 9, Section 1
Oklahoma   6% Oklahoma Statutes, 1961, Title 15,
                       Section 266
Oregon   6% Oregon Revised Statutes, Section 82.010
Pennsylvania   6% Purdon's Pennsylvania Statutes Annotated,
                       Title 41, Section 3
Puerto Rico   6% Laws of Puerto Rico Annotated, Title 31,
                       Section 3025
Rhode Island   6% Rhode Island General Laws of 1956,
                       Section 6.26.1
South Carolina 6% Code of Laws of South Carolina, 1962,
                       Title 8 Section 3
South Dakota   6% South Dakota Code of 1939, Title 38,
                       Chapter 1, Section 8
Tennessee   6% Official Tennessee Code Annotated (1956)
                       Section 47-1604
Texas   6% Vernon's Texas Statutes of 1948, Article 5071
Utah   6% Utah Code Annotated, 1953, Title 15,
                       Section 1-1
Vermont   6% Vermont Statutes Annotated, Title 9,
                       Section 31
Virginia   6% Code of Virginia, Title 6, Section 346
Virgin Islands   6% Virgin Islands Code, Title 11, Section 951
Washington   6% Revised Code of Washington, Section
                       19.52.010
West Virginia   6% Michie's West Virginia Code of 1951,
                       Annotated, Chapter 47, Article 6,
                       Section 5
Wisconsin   5% Wisconsin Statutes, 1965, Chapter 115,
                       Section 4
Wyoming   7% Wyoming Statutes, 1957, Title 13,
                       Section 477

The lowest legal interest rate is that of North Dakota (4 per cent), followed by Illinois, Iowa, Louisiana, Michigan, and Wisconsin, all five of which use 5 per cent as their legal interest rate.

The legislatures of California, Georgia, Nevada, and Wyoming have created the highest legal interest rates in the nation, 7 per cent.

By far the largest number of statutes analyzed, 43 in all, adopt 6 per cent as their legal rate.

Maximum Interest Rates

The chart that follows attempts to present the maximum interest rates established by the legislatures of 53 jurisdictions as they apply to secured second mortgage loans.

MAXIMUM INTEREST RATES

(**NOTE:** The interest rates cited are not to be regarded as the limit of earnings available to a mortgage investor.

In an 8 per cent interest state, for example, an investor might purchase an existing bona fide mortgage from the original mortgagee at a discount. The net return might then be 10, 12, or even 16 per cent.

Corporate mortgages, particularly in low interest states, are often not limited by maximum interest rates. See the third chart, "Are Corporations Excluded?")

Alabama	8%	Alabama Code, 1958, Title 9, Section 60
		Interest up to six per cent per annum for entire period of loan may be computed in advance and added to principal even though loan is to be repaid in monthly or other installments. Title 9, Section 61, as amended by 1953 Session Law 554.
Alaska	8%	Alaska Statutes 1962, 45.45.010
Arizona	8%	Arizona Revised Statutes, 1956, Section 44.1201
Arkansas	10%	Arkansas Statutes 1957, 68.602
California	15%	4% in fees. California Code Chapter 8, Article 2, Section 3081.1 et cetera
Colorado	24% with Lic.	12% without license; Colorado Revised Statutes 1963, Chapter 73, Article 2, Section 5

Connecticut	12%	Connecticut General Statutes, 1958, Section 37-4 No limit on mortgages above $5,000
Delaware	6%	Delaware Code, Title 6, Section 2301.2304
D.C.	8%	Code of District of Columbia, 1961, Section 28-3301
Florida	10%	Corporations may pay 15%. Florida Statutes 1965, Section 687.01-02
Georgia	8%	Code of Georgia Annotated, Section 57-101
Hawaii	12%	Revised Laws of Hawaii, 1955, Chapter 191
Idaho	8%	Idaho Code 27-1904,6
Illinois	7%	Illinois Revised Statutes, 1965, Chapter 74, Section 4
Indiana	8%	Burns' Indiana Statutes Annotated of 1933, Title 19, Chapter 20, Section 1
Iowa	7%	Code of Iowa, 1962, Chapter 535, Section 2 as amended in 1963, Chapter 317, Section 1
Kansas	10%	Kansas Statutes Annotated, 1965, Chapter 16, Article 202, as amended, 1965
Kentucky	6%	Kentucky Revised Statutes, Official Edition 1964, 360.010
Louisiana	8%	Civil Code, Revision of 1870, Article 2924
Maine	No Limit	Maine Revised Statutes Annotated, 1964, Title 9, Section 228
Maryland	6%	Michie's Code, 1957 Edition, Article 49, Section 1
Massachusetts	18%	1959 Session Laws, Chapter 505, 1960 Session Laws, Chapter 446; 1962 Session Laws, Chapters 286 and 523
Michigan	7%	Compiled Laws of 1948 & Masons' 1961 Supplement thereto, Section 438.51
Minnesota	8%	Minnesota Statutes, 1961, Chapter 334, Section 1
Mississippi	8%	Mississippi Code of 1942
Missouri	8%	Missouri Revised Statutes, 1959, Section 408.030
Montana	10%	Revised Codes of Montana, 1947, Title 47-12-5
Nebraska	9%	Revised Statutes of Nebraska, 1943, Section 45-102
Nevada	12%	Nevada Revised Statutes, Sections 99.040, 99.050

New Hampshire	18%	New Hampshire Revised Statutes Annotated 1955 Chapter 336, Section 1
New Jersey	14%	Statutes Annotated, Section 31:1-1 and Section 17:11A
New Mexico	10%	New Mexico Statutes Annotated 1953, Chapter 50, Section 6-16
New York	6%	General Obligation Law Section 5-501(2)
North Carolina	6%	+10% of mortgage loan, Chapter 45, Section 43.1 General Statutes of North Carolina
North Dakota	7%	North Dakota, Century Code Annotated Section 14-09, Chapter 47
Ohio	8%	+Service Charge of 5% or $200, whichever is less, Baldwin's Ohio Revised Code Annotated 1953, Chapter 13, Title 21, Section 57
Oklahoma	10%	Oklahoma Statutes 1961, Title 15, Section 266
Oregon	10%	and for corporations other than charitable, religious or nonprofit, 12%, Oregon Revised Statutes, Section 708.480
Pennsylvania	6%	Purdon's Pennsylvania Statutes Annotated, Title 41, Section 3
Puerto Rico	9%	Up to $3,000, 9%; over $3,000, 8%
Rhode Island	30%	Rhode Island General Laws of 1956, Section 6.26.1
South Carolina	7%	Code of Laws of South Carolina 1962, Title 8 Section 3
South Dakota	8%	South Dakota Code of 1939, 1960 Supplement
Tennessee	6%	Official Tennessee Code Annotated (1956) Section 47-1605
Texas	10%	Vernon's Texas Statutes of 1948, Article 5071
Utah	14%	Utah Code Annotated 1953, Title 15, Section 1-2 10% + additional charges (4% service charge). Under $5,000, limit 14%. 1953 Session Laws, Chapter 24; 1955 Session Laws, Chapter 20, Title 15, Section 1-2
Vermont	6%	Vermont Statutes Annotated, Title 8, Section 3001
Virginia	6%	Code of Virginia, Title 6, Section 347
Virgin Islands	10%	Virgin Islands Code, Title 11, Section 951

Washington	12% Revised Code of Washington, Section 19.52.010
West Virginia	6% Michie's West Virginia Code of 1951, Annotated
Wisconsin	12% Wisconsin Statutes, 1965, Chapter 115, Section 5(1)
Wyoming	10% Wyoming Statutes, 1957, Title 13, Section 476

The median maximum interest rate falls between 9 per cent and 10 per cent.

The average maximum interest rate is 10 per cent.

Of the fifty-three jurisdictions examined, twenty-six permit a charge of 10 per cent or more.

Of the twenty-seven jurisdictions limiting the maximum permissible interest to rates below 10 per cent, eighteen exclude corporations from the limitation.

Of those states limiting the maximum interest rate to 6 per cent, only two, Tennessee and Vermont, do not exclude corporations from the protection of the usury statutes.

Every state limiting the maximum interest rate to 7 per cent excludes corporations from the protection of the usury laws.

Seven of the twelve states limiting the maximum interest rate to 8 per cent exclude corporations from the protection of the usury statutes.

Are Corporations Excluded?

Where the exclusion exists, bona fide corporate borrowers are denied the protection of interest limits.

Alabama	No.
Alaska	No.
Arizona	Corporations cannot claim usury on interest rates up to 12 per cent for loans over $3,500 where agreed to in writing and authorized by its Board of Directors. Excluded are public, charitable, religious, non-profit, and those corporations whose principal asset is a one- or two-family dwelling. Arizona Revised Statutes, 1956, Section 10-177.

Arkansas	No.
California	No.
Colorado	No.
Connecticut	No.
Delaware	Corporations, including associations and joint stock companies possessing any of the privileges and powers of corporations not enjoyed by individuals, may not utilize the defense of usury. Delaware Code, Title 6, Section 2306.
D.C.	No.
Florida	No, although corporate interest rate is higher. See chart, Maximum Interest Rates.
Georgia	Corporations organized for profit may contract for any interest rate on loans which, originally or by renewal or extension, exceed $2,500. Defense of usury not available. Code of Georgia Annotated, Section 57-118.
Hawaii	No.
Idaho	No.
Illinois	Where corporation is debtor, any rate is permitted in written contract or on a loan to a business association, copartnership, sole proprietorship, limited partnership, or trustee, solely for the purpose of carrying on business. Illinois Revised Statutes, 1965, Chapter 74, Section 4.
Indiana	Corporations by written contract may agree to pay any rate. Burns' Indiana Statutes Annotated of 1933, Title 19, Chapter 20, Section 1.
Iowa	Corporations may contract to pay more than statutory maximum. Code of Iowa, 1962, Chapter 525, Section 2, as amended in 1963, Chapter 317, Section 1.
Kansas	Defense of usury not available to corporations, Kansas Statutes Annotated, 1965, Chapter 17, Article 4103.
Kentucky	Corporations may not plead usury as a defense. Kentucky Revised Statutes, Official Edition, 1964, 360.025.
Louisiana	Corporations organized for profit may agree to pay any rate of interest. Louisiana Revised Statutes of 1950, Title 12, Section 603.
Maine	No limit for corporations or individuals.

Maryland	Corporations may not plead usury as a defense. Michie's Code, 1957 Edition, Article 23, Section 125.
Massachusetts	No.
Michigan	Usury cannot be pleaded by a corporation organized for profit. Compiled Laws of 1948 & Masons' 1961 Supplement thereto, Section 450.78.
Minnesota	Corporations are forbidden to interpose the defense of usury. Minnesota Statutes, 1961, Chapter 334, Section 21.
Mississippi	No.
Missouri	Corporations cannot interpose defense of usury. Missouri Revised Statutes, 1959, Section 408.060.
Montana	No.
Nebraska	Corporations, by written agreement, may exceed the legal rate. Revised Statutes of Nebraska, 1943, Section 45-102.
Nevada	No.
New Hampshire	No.
New Jersey	Corporations may not plead usury. Statutes Annotated, Section 31:1-1.
New Mexico	No.
New York	Corporations (other than those whose principal asset is a one- or two-family dwelling) and associations or joint stock companies having corporate privileges and powers may not interpose defense of usury. General Obligation Law Section 5-521.
North Carolina	Private corporations may enter into contracts to borrow money and pay a charge not exceeding 6 per cent of the original loan amount for each 12 months of the loan's duration even though loan is payable in installments. General Statutes of North Carolina, Chapter 24, Section 2. Loans over $30,000, corporations may pay 8 per cent.
North Dakota	No.
Ohio	Corporations may not plead usury. Baldwin's Ohio Revised Code Annotated 1953, Chapter 17, Title 1, Section 68.
Oklahoma	No.

Oregon	Yes, up to 12 per cent. Oregon Revised Statutes, Section 708.480.
Pennsylvania	Certain corporations may not plead usury. Purdon's Pennsylvania Statutes Annotated, Title 41, Section 2.
Puerto Rico	No.
Rhode Island	No.
South Carolina	Business corporations with par value stock or stated capital of $40,000 cannot plead usury. Code of Laws of South Carolina 1962, Title 8, Section 8.
South Dakota	No.
Tennessee	No.
Texas	No.
Vermont	No.
Virginia	Corporations may not plead usury. Code of Virginia, Title 6, Section 357.
Virgin Islands	No.
Washington	No.
West Virginia	Corporations may not plead usury. Michie's West Virginia Code of 1951, Annotated, Chapter 47, Article 6, Section 10.
Wisconsin	No.
Wyoming	No.

Recognizing Realities

Thus, the applicable statutes indicate that the realities of the market place are recognized in one form or another.

The price of money cannot be limited to 6 per cent. Money is simply a more expensive commodity. The law is not blind. If it imposes an unrealistic limit in one area, it inevitably permits realism to triumph in other areas.

Excluding corporations from the protection of usury laws is but one method.

Permitting a limited amount of fees to be charged is another means of recognizing reality.

Unless lawful means are made available to legitimate businessmen who seek to invest their funds, they will withdraw from the jurisdiction. The need for funds will still remain—and, unfortunately, the vacuum left by honorable investors will be filled by unscrupulous money lenders.

One View

The *New York Times,* in a detailed report of New York's recent review of usury laws by the New York State Banking Department, Attorney General's office, the Governor's legal staff, and the State Investigation Commission, reported:

> Some students of the problem question whether the state should set maximum interest rates at all, especially on business loans. Ceilings are essentially arbitrary, they say, and tend to curtail the flow of credit from legitimate sources to would-be entrepreneurs.

> One idea being considered in the State Banking Department is to allow rates of up to 40 per cent on loans of more than $3,000. The object would be to make high-risk loans available from reputable lenders by permitting a rate of return commensurate with the risk.

I do not quote this report in an effort to champion to elimination of all restraints. It does seem reasonable, though, if the State Banking Department of the State of New York could seriously entertain maximum rates of 40 per cent, to gently remind one and all that realistic interest rates will provide infinitely more protection to a borrower than artificially depressed limits.

The Need For Writing

The following chart tabulates whether or not state legislatures have decreed that a written contract is necessary in order to effectively utilize the maximum legal interest rate.

IF ABOVE LEGAL RATE, NEED CONTRACT BE IN WRITING?

Alabama	Yes	Alabama Code, 1958, Title 9, Section 60
Alaska	No	Alaska Statutes 1962, Section 45.45.010
Arizona	Yes	Arizona Revised Statutes, 1956, Section 44-1201
Arkansas	Yes	Arkansas Statutes, 1957, Section 68.602
California	Yes	California Constitution, Article XX, Section 22

Colorado	Yes	Colorado Revised Statutes, 1963, Section 73-1-3
Connecticut	No	Connecticut General Statutes, 1958, Section 37-4
Delaware		Legal rate is maximum rate
D.C.	Yes	Code of District of Columbia, 1961, Section 28-3301
Florida	Yes	Florida Statutes, 1965, Section 687.01-.02
Georgia	Yes	Code of Georgia Annotated, Section 57-101
Hawaii	Yes	Revised Laws of Hawaii, 1955, Chapter 191
Idaho	Yes	Idaho Code, 1947, Section 27-1094-6, Chapter 16, Article 202
Illinois	Yes	Illinois Revised Statutes 1965, Chapter 74, Section 4
Indiana	Yes	Burns' Indiana Statutes Annotated of 1933, Title 19, Chapter 20, Section 1
Iowa	Yes	Code of Iowa, 1967, Chapter 535, Section 2, As amended in 1963, Chapter 317, Section 1
Kansas	Yes	Kansas Statutes Annotated, 1965
Kentucky		Legal Rate is maximum rate
Louisiana	No	Civil Code Revision of 1870, Article 2924
Maine	Yes	Maine Revised Statutes Annotated, 1964, Title 9, Section 228
Maryland		Legal rate is maximum rate
Massachusetts	Yes	1959 Session Laws, Chapter 505; 1960 Session Laws, Chapter 446; 1962 Session Laws, Chapters 286 and 523
Michigan	Yes	Compiled Laws of 1948 & Masons' 1961 Supplement thereto, Section 438.51
Minnesota	Yes	Minnesota Statutes, 1961, Chapter 334, Section 1
Mississippi	Yes	Mississippi Code of 1942, Section 36
Missouri	Yes	Missouri Revised Statutes, 1959, Section 408.030
Montana	Yes	Revised Code of Montana, 1947, Title 47-12-5
Nebraska	Yes	Revised Statutes of Nebraska, 1943, Section 45-102
Nevada	Yes	Nevada Revised Statutes, Section 99.040-99.050
New Hampshire	Yes	New Hampshire Revised Statutes Annotated 1955 Chapter 336, Section 1

New Jersey		Legal rate is maximum rate.
New Mexico	Yes	New Mexico Statutes Annotated 1953, Chapter 50, Section 6-16
New York		Legal rate is maximum rate
North Carolina	No	
North Dakota	Yes	North Dakota, Century Code Annotated, Section 14-09, Chapter 47
Ohio	Yes	Baldwin's Ohio Revised Code Annotated 1953, Chapter 13, Title 9, Section 1-3
Oklahoma	Yes	Oklahoma Statutes 1961, Title 15, Section 266
Oregon	Yes	Oregon Revised Statutes, Section 708.480
Pennsylvania		Legal rate is maximum rate
Puerto Rico	Yes	Laws of Puerto Rico Annotated, Title 31, Section 3025
Rhode Island	Yes	Rhode Island General Laws of 1956, Section 6.26.1-2
South Carolina	Yes	Code of Laws of South Carolina 1962, Title 8, Section 3.
South Dakota	Yes	1960 Supplement to Code of 1939
Tennessee		Legal rate is maximum rate
Texas	Yes	Vernon's Texas Statutes of 1948, Article 5701
Utah	Yes	Utah Code Annotated 1953, Title 15, Section 1-2
Vermont		Legal rate is maximum rate
Virginia		Legal rate is maximum rate
Virgin Islands	Yes	Virgin Islands Code, Title 11, Section 951
Washington	Yes	Revised Code of Washington, Section 19.52.010
West Virginia		Legal rate is maximum rate
Wisconsin	Yes	Wisconsin Statutes, 1965, Chapter 115, Section 5(4)
Wyoming	No	

The Penalties for Usury

In the vast majority of jurisdictions analyzed, penalties are imposed upon parties to usurious loans.

An analysis follows.

PENALTIES FOR EXCEEDING PERMISSIBLE
INTEREST RATES (USURY)

Alabama	Forfeiture of all interest. All interest paid is deducted from principal. Alabama Code, 1958, Title 9, Section 65.
Alaska	Forfeiture of all interest. Persons paying usurious interest may recover double that amount by action brought within two years. Alaska Statutes 1962, Section 45.45.030.
Arizona	Forfeiture of all interest. All usurious payments are applied to principal. Arizona Revised Statutes, 1956, Section 44-1202.3.
Arkansas	Both principal and interest are forfeited. Arkansas Constitution, Article 19, Section 13. Usurious contracts can be cancelled without tender of any part of the debt. Creditors may attack usurious loans and conveyances. Arkansas Statutes, 1957, Section 68.609-611.
California	Forfeiture of all interest. Triple the amount of interest over 10 per cent may be recovered. General Laws Act 3757, Section 3.
Colorado	Treble damages plus costs of suit if action brought within one year. Colorado Revised Statutes, 1963, Section 73-2-9.
Connecticut	Forfeit principal and interest. Connecticut General Statutes, 1958, Section 36-243, Section 37-8.
Delaware	Forfeiture of excess interest over permissible rate. If paid, excess can be recovered within one year of payment. Delaware Code, Title 6, Section 2304.
D.C.	Forfeiture of interest. Usurious interest paid may be recovered. Code of the District of Columbia, 1961, Section 28-3303,4.
Florida	Forfeiture of all interest. Where paid, double interest forfeited. Florida Statutes, 1965, Section 687.04. Where interest exceeds 25 per cent, principal and interest are both forfeited. Lender guilty of misdemeanor. Florida Statutes 1965, Section 687.07.
Georgia	Forfeiture of all interest. Where paid, may be recovered by suit brought within one year. Code of Georgia Annotated, Section 57-112, 115.
Hawaii	Forfeiture of all interest. Revised Laws of Hawaii, 1955, Chapter 191, Section 4.

Idaho	Forfeiture of all interest. Interest paid, plus twice the amount of said interest, may be recovered. Idaho Code, Section 27-1907.
Illinois	Forfeit twice the total of all interest, discount and charges determined by the loan, or paid by obligor, whichever is greater, plus attorney's fees and court costs. Illinois Revised Statutes, 1965, Chapter 74, Section 6.
Indiana	Where interest contracted for exceeds 8 per cent interest paid or reserved in excess of 6 per cent may be recovered. Burns' Indiana Statutes Annotated of 1933, Title 19, Chapter 20, Section 4.
Iowa	Plaintiff granted judgment only for principal, forfeiting interest and costs. Judgment entered against defendant in favor of the state for 8 per cent per annum on judgment amount. Code of Iowa, 1962, Chapter 535, Section 5.
Kansas	Forfeit all interest and charges in excess of those permitted, and, as a penalty, forfeit an amount equal to interest and charges contracted for in excess of permissible rates. Kansas Statutes Annotated 1965, Chapter 16, Article 202, as amended in 1965.
Kentucky	Forfeit interest in excess of permissible rate. Excess recoverable if action brought within one year of payment. Kentucky Revised Statutes, Official Edition, 1964, 360.020, 413.040.
Louisiana	May recover usurious interest by suit within two years of payment. Civil Code, Revision of 1870, Article 2924. Conflict unresolved as to whether forfeit excess interest or all interest.
Maine	None. No maximum interest limit.
Maryland	Forfeit excess over real sum advanced and the legal interest on such sum. Michie's Code, 1957 Edition, Article 49, Section 4.
Massachusetts	No general usury law.
Michigan	Forfeit all interest. Compiled Laws of 1948 and Masons' 1961 Supplement thereto, Section 438.52 et seq.
Minnesota	Contract void, court may enjoin all proceedings thereon, and order its cancellation and surrender. Minnesota Statutes, 1961, Chapter 334, Sections

	3 and 5, as amended in 1965, Chapter 391. If paid, usurious interest may be recovered, with costs, provided action initiated within two years. One-half of recovery paid into county treasury. Minnesota Statutes, 1961, Chapter 334, Section 2.
Mississippi	Forfeit all interest. If rate greater than 20 per cent, forfeit principal. Interest paid may be recovered. If rate exceeds 20 per cent, principal and interest may be recovered. Mississippi Code of 1942.
Missouri	Creditor may recover six per cent interest instead of contract rate. Excess over legal rate applied on principal or debtor can recover excess with reasonable attorney's fee and costs. Missouri Revised Statutes 1959, Section 408-060.
Montana	Forfeit doublt interest. When paid, may be recovered by action brought within two years. Revised Codes of Montana 1947, Title 47, Chapter 12, Section 6.
Nebraska	Forfeit interest. Revised Statutes of Nebraska, 1943, Section 45-105.
Nevada	Forfeit excess interest. Nevada Revised Statutes, Section 99.030. No provisions for recovery of usury paid.
New Hampshire	No general usury law.
New Jersey	Forfeit interest and costs. Liable to $1,000 penalty.
New Mexico	Forfeit interest. If paid, can recover double amount by suit within two years. New Mexico Statutes Annotated, 1953, Chapter 50, Section 6-18. Usury is misdemeanor. Chapter 50, Section 6-19.
New York	Forfeit principal and interest. General Obligation Law Section 5-511. May recover excess interest within one year of payment. Section 5-513.
North Carolina	Forfeiture of all interest. If paid, may recover double interest amount by suit within two years. General Statutes of North Carolina, Chapter 1, Section 53; Chapter 6, Section 25; Chapter 24, Section 1-7.
North Dakota	Forfeiture of all interest and 25 per cent of principal. Where paid, may recover double interest

and 25 per cent of principal within four years of date of transaction. North Dakota, Century Code Annotated, 1953, Section 47-14-10. Usury is a misdemeanor, Section 47-14-11.

Ohio	If charge is greater than 8 per cent, payments in excess of 6 per cent are applied to debt. Baldwin's Ohio Revised Code Annotated, 1953, Chapter 13, Title 9, Section 4.
Oklahoma	Forfeiture of double the interest. Attorney's fees taxed as costs for prevailing party. Oklahoma Statutes, 1961, Title 15, Section 267-8.
Oregon	Entire debt forfeited to school fund of county where suit brought. Oregon Revised Statutes, Section 82.120.
Pennsylvania	Debtor cannot be required to pay excess over legal rates. When paid, may be recovered if suit brought within six months. Purdon's Pennsylvania Statutes Annotated, Title 41, Section 4.
Puerto Rico	Forfeit of interest and 25 per cent of principal, which is awarded to people of Puerto Rico. Laws of Puerto Rico Annotated, Title 31, Section 3025.
Rhode Island	Forfeit of principal and interest. Rhode Island General Laws of 1956, Section 6-26-4.
South Carolina	Forfeit all interest and costs of the action. When paid, double interest forfeited. Code of Laws of South Carolina, 1962, Title 8, Section 5.
South Dakota	Where 8 per cent maximum interest applies, forfeit all excess. 1960 Supplement to Code of 1939.
Tennessee	Usurious on face, contract void. Otherwise, usurious portion void. When paid, may be recovered if suit brought within two years. Official Tennessee Code Annotated (1956) Section 47-1604, 1612, 1615, 1617.
Texas	Forfeit of all interest. Interest paid may be recovered in double the amount. Vernon's Texas Statutes of 1948, Article 5071, 5073.
Utah	Forfeiture of entire interest due. If paid, triple the sum recoverable plus attorney's fees if suit initiated within two years. Utah Code Annotated, 1953, Title 15, Section 1-7. Misdemeanor. Title 15, Section 1-5.

Vermont   Forfeiture of interest exceeding 6 per cent.
                 Knowingly or willfully loaning at usurious rate
                 carries loss of all interest and one-half of prin-
                 cipal. Misdemeanor. Vermont Statutes Annotated,
                 Title 9, Section 34(c).

Virginia   Forfeiture of all interest. If paid, excess may be
                 recovered if action begun within one year. Code
                 of Virginia, Title 6, Section 350.

Virgin Islands   Forfeiture of all interest. If paid, double the
                 amount may be recovered if action begun within
                 two years. Virgin Islands Code, Title 11, Section
                 953, 954.

Washington   Recovery limited to principal less accrued interest
                 and defendant's costs. If paid, recover double
                 the amount. Revised Code of Washington, Sec-
                 tion 19,52.030.

West Virginia   Forfeit excess above legal rate. If paid, credited
                 to principal. Michie's West Virginia Code of
                 1951, Annotated, Section 47, Article 6, Section
                 6.7.

Wisconsin   Forfeit all interest and up to $2,000 of principal
                 if action brought within two years. Fine and up
                 to six months imprisonment. Wisconsin Statutes,
                 1965, Chapter 115, Section 6.

Wyoming   Forfeit all interest and costs of suit. Any interest
                 paid is deducted. Wyoming Statutes, 1957 Title
                 13, Section 482.

12

Charting Monthly Payments

Variations ... Loan Amortization Schedules ... Compute-It-Yourself ... Available Aids ... Sample Payment Tables ...Build a Library ... Interpolation ... Other Payment Chart Uses ... Accuracy

Variations

First, let's examine the word "monthly." Are payments on a regular monthly basis an absolute requirement? Not really. The methods of payment are limited only by the ingenuity of man.

Payments could be made every two months, quarterly, semi-annually, or annually. You might elect to accept interest only, postponing any payments towards principal for one month, two, four, or six months before calling for payments combining both principal and interest.

You might permit the mortgagor to set his own pattern of repayment of principal to meet his fluctuating financial situations, insisting only upon regular interest payments.

But, please, do not misunderstand. The range of possibilities is infinitely wider than the range of wisdom.

Learn to walk before you try to tango. Don't explode upon the financial scene with dazzling, daring footwork. You just might trip.

Hybrid payment patterns, skipping hither and yon over the calendar, are as foolish as they are complicated. Keep it simple. Keep it direct. Keep it constant.

It takes some people months to learn that they now have a new mortgage payment to make every thirty days. They sometimes meet their $44.49 payment with a check for $40.49, or $44.00. Occasionally they magnanimously forward $45.00 a month. "Say, Gloria, what did you say that new payment was? I forgot."

Sometimes they forget that first payment completely.

If they have trouble remembering constant amounts on repetitive dates, how in heaven's name can you expect them to remember a fluctuating amount on sporadic dates?

Keep it simple.

Loan Amortization Schedules

The technique that is best suited for your purpose is the use of a loan amortization schedule. Such a schedule indicates the specific monthly payment which, when applied as partial payments of principal and full payments of the monthly interest due on the declining principal amount, will amortize or extinguish the entire loan in a given period of time.

How does it work?

Let's take a simple example, a $1,500 loan to be amortized by equal monthly payments over a period of four years. The loan in this sample will carry a simple interest rate of 12 per cent per annum.

Payments will be $39.51 per month for 48 months, the final payment, the forty-eighth, will be $38.92.

$1,500.00 Loan, four years, 12 per cent Interest, $39.51 Payments:

Payment	Amount Applied to Interest	Amount Applied to Principal	Loan Balance
1	$15.00	$24.51	$1,475.49
2	14.75	24.76	1,450.73
3	14.51	25.00	1,425.73
4	14.26	25.25	1,400.48
5	14.00	25.51	1,374.97
6	13.78	25.76	1,349.21
7	13.49	26.02	1,323.19

Payment	Amount Applied to Interest	Amount Applied to Principal	Loan Balance
8	13.23	26.28	1,296.91
9	12.97	26.54	1,270.37
10	12.70	26.81	1,243.56
11	12.44	27.07	1,216.49
12	12.16	27.35	1,189.14
13	11.89	27.62	1,161.52
14	11.62	27.89	1,133.63
15	11.34	28.17	1,105.46
16	11.05	28.46	1,077.00
17	10.77	28.74	1,043.26
18	10.48	29.03	1,019.23
19	10.19	29.32	989.91
20	9.90	29.61	960.30
21	9.60	29.91	930.39
22	9.30	30.21	900.18
23	9.00	30.51	869.67
24	8.78	30.81	838.86
25	8.39	31.12	807.74
26	8.08	31.43	776.31
27	7.76	31.75	744.56
28	7.45	32.06	712.50
29	7.13	32.38	680.12
30	6.80	32.71	647.41
31	6.47	33.04	614.37
32	6.14	33.37	581.00
33	5.81	33.70	547.30
34	5.47	34.04	513.26
35	5.13	34.38	478.88
36	4.79	34.72	444.16
37	4.44	35.07	409.09
38	4.09	35.42	373.67
39	3.74	35.77	337.90

Payment	Amount Applied to Interest	Amount Applied to Principal	Loan Balance
40	3.38	36.13	301.77
41	3.02	36.49	265.28
42	2.65	36.86	228.42
43	2.28	37.23	191.19
44	1.91	37.60	153.59
45	1.54	37.97	115.62
46	1.16	38.35	77.27
47	.77	38.74	38.53
48	.39	38:53	38.92

Now that we have seen what a typical Loan Amortization Schedule, or a Loan Reduction Chart, looks like, I think it would be worthwhile to analyze it.

Compute-It-Yourself

If you knew the monthly payment necessary to reduce the $1,500, 12 per cent, four-year loan, you would have all the information necessary to compute the reduction chart yourself.

How?

Twelve per cent simple interest is 1 per cent a month on the outstanding balance of the loan. One per cent of the initial balance, $1,500, is $15.00. If you know that the monthly payment to be applied to the reduction of the loan is $39.51, deduct the necessary interest payments, fifteen dollars, from $39.51, and the balance available to reduce the principal of the loan is $24.51.

Thus, the first payment would result in a principal balance of $1,475.49.

Monthly payment	$39.51
1 per cent of $1,500.00 (interest due)	– 15.00
Available to reduce principal	$24.51
Initial principal	$1,500.00
First payment to reduce principal	– 24.51
New principal balance	$1,475.49

The second payment would not be divided into $15.00 and $24.51. A larger share would be applied to principal.

Why? Because the principal has been reduced from $1,500.00 to $1,475.49. The interest due on the new balance at the rate of one per cent a month would now come to only $14.75, or $.25 less than the first installment of interest. Because the total monthly payment remains constant, the twenty-five cents that is no longer required for the interest portion will be applied to the principal portion.

Monthly payment	$39.51
One per cent of $1,475.49 (interest due)	−14.75
Available to reduce principal	$24.76
Current principal balance	$1,475.49
Second payment to reduce principal	− 24.76
New principal balance	$1,450.73

This pattern is repeated forty-eight times, always deducting one per cent of the current mortgage loan balance from the monthly payment, and applying the balance of the monthly payment to reduce the principal.

Regardless of the interest rate charges, the length of the loan, or the dollar amount of the loan, each monthly payment will result in a smaller interest payment and a larger principal payment—providing the monthly payment is in excess of the initial monthly interest charge.

This approach will apply to any interest rate. At six per cent simple interest per annum, the monthly interest rate is one-half of one per cent. At nine per cent simple interest, the monthly interest rate is three-quarters of one per cent, or .0075.

Available Aids

The Financial Publishing Company, 82 Brookline Avenue, Boston, Massachusetts, 02215, publishes payment tables for monthly mortgage loans, showing the monthly payments required to amortize a loan in a given period of time.

One booklet published by them, typical of the wide range of assistance available, indicates the monthly payments resulting from interest rates of four and a half to seven per cent at intervals of one-fourth per cent, on amounts from $100 to $20,000, at intervals of $100, as well as annual terms from one year to 40 years.

They produce thick tomes, carrying longer ranges of interest, shorter intervals of loan amounts, and terms varying by less than annual periods.

The booklet you would find most practical is one limited to interest rates prevailing in your community. It will report the monthly payments required for one dollar to five thousand dollars at one dollar intervals to the tenth dollar, ten dollar intervals to the hundredth dollar, and fifty dollar intervals thereafter. It groups those payments at 6, 12, 18, 24, 30, 36, 42, 48, 54, 60, 72, 84, 96, 108, and 120 months.

Sample Payment Tables

To indicate the manner in which payment tables are organized, I have excerpted some computations. They are not the same fine divisions found in the bound tables, but they will be sufficient to indicate the manner in which the material is presented.

Eight per cent

Amount of Loan	24 Monthly Payments	36 Monthly Payments	48 Monthly Payments	60 Monthly Payments
$1,500	$ 67.85	$ 47.01	$ 36.62	$ 30.42
2,000	90.46	62.68	48.83	40.56
2,500	113.07	78.35	61.04	50.70
3,000	135.69	94.01	73.24	60.83
3,500	158.30	109.68	85.45	70.97
4,000	180.91	125.35	97.66	81.11
4,500	203.53	141.02	109.86	91.25
5,000	226.14	156.69	122.07	101.39

Ten per cent

Amount of Loan	24 Monthly Payments	36 Monthly Payments	48 Monthly Payments	60 Monthly Payments
$1,500	$ 69.22	$ 48.41	$ 38.05	$ 31.88
2,000	92.29	64.54	50.73	42.50
2,500	115.37	80.67	63.41	53.12
3,000	138.44	96.81	76.09	63.75
3,500	161.51	112.94	88.77	74.37
4,000	184.58	129.07	101.46	84.99
4,500	207.66	145.21	114.14	95.62
5,000	230.73	161.34	126.82	106.24

Amount of Loan	24 Monthly Payments	36 Monthly Payments Twelve per cent	48 Monthly Payments	60 Monthly Payments
$1,500	$ 70.62	$ 49.83	$ 39.51	$ 33.37
2,000	94.15	66.43	52.67	44.49
2,500	117.69	83.04	65.84	55.62
3,000	141.23	99.65	79.01	66.74
3,500	164.76	116.26	92.17	77.86
4,000	188.30	132.86	105.34	88.98
4,500	211.84	149.47	118.51	100.11
5,000	235.37	166.08	131.67	111.23

At a true annual interest rate of eight per cent, the monthly payment required to extinguish a loan of $2,500 in 48 months is $61.04.

At 10 per cent, a man who can afford to commit himself to a payment of approximately $65.00 could borrow $2,000 for three years, $2,500 for four years, or $3,000 for five years.

At 12 per cent, a man needing $1500 could choose between monthly payments of $70.62, $49.83, $39.51, or $33.37.

Build a Library

These sources of monthly payments are a necessary sales tool.

No one with whom you would be willing to deal would borrow $1,500 for three years without knowing the payments required.

Without being familiar with the necessary monthly payments, you could not evaluate your prospective mortgagor's ability to pay.

Unless they are armed with the monthly costs, the parties cannot choose a loan schedule best suited to their needs.

Without a payment table, the investor cannot compare costs of second mortgages with refinancing the first mortgage (see Chapter 4) or borrowing from a small loan company.

An adequate library of payment schedules is a necessity. Fortunately, two booklets will prove adequate. I suggest you purchase one that carries a range of interest rates similar to those common to your community. Add a second, and smaller, booklet dealing in minute detail with the current second mortgage interest rate in your community. The cost will be refreshingly modest.

Interpolation

What if the borrower's needs are not reflected in your payment tables? He does not want to borrow a nickel more than he needs, and he needs seventeen hundred eighty-five dollars. You have the figures for $1,500, and the monthly payments required for $2,000. What do you do now?

Interpolate.

Two thousand dollars cost $64.54 for three years at 10 per cent. Fifteen hundred dollars cost $48.41.

The difference is $16.13.

The spread between $1,500 and $2,000 is $500. The spread between $1,785 and $1,500 is $285, or 57 per cent of $500.

Fifty-seven per cent of $16.13 is $9.19. Forty-eight dollars and forty-one cents plus $9.19, is $57.60.

Thus the cost of $1,785 for three years at 10 per cent annual interest is $57.60.

```
$2,000 = $64.54 per month        $1,785
-1,500 = -48.41 per month        -1,500                    .57
$  500    $16.13                  $  285         500 | 285.00
                                                       250 0
                                                        35 00
                                                        35 00
                                                            0

  $16.13           $285  = $ 9.19
   x.57            1,500  =  48.41
  1.1291           $1,785 = $57.60 per month
  8.065
  $9.1941
```

For those who find the intricacies of interpolation too strenuous, simple addition will often solve the problem. Find the monthly payments for $1,700 and $85 in your mortgage booklet and add them together.

You need not really be precise at this early stage. The applicant will accept a reasonable approximation, providing you can produce the exact figure prior to the final meeting.

If the amount is clearly set forth in a printed payment chart, no problem exists. The applicant can study the chart and see for himself how the monthly cost was chosen.

Other Payment Chart Uses

Interest charges are tax deductible. How will your mortgagor know what portion of each monthly payment has been applied to interest? Will either of you have the patience to compute the monthly fluctuations?

The interest earned is taxable income. How will you know how much income to declare?

At some time during the life of the mortgage, your mortgagor may choose to pay the balance in full and terminate the loan. What is the balance due on a three-year, $1,500, 10 per cent mortgage loan 14 months and six days after it has been initiated?

You may have accumulated some additional funds and find yourself eager to renew a 21-month old mortgage back to its original principal amount for a particularly prompt and well-secured borrower. How much more money should you advance?

The problems are complex.

Fortunately, the solution are simple. If you have not already done so, order a loan amortization schedule.

As you have seen, a mortgage reduction schedule, or loan amortization schedule, itemizes the portion of each monthly payment applied to principal and to interest. It details the precise loan balance remaining after each monthly payment is made.

Let's go back to the problem of computing the balance due on a mortgage fourteen months and six days after it has been initiated. Finding the fourteen month figure is simple. Just use line number fourteen on the schedule. The fourteenth line of the balance of loan balance column contains the mortgage balance after fourteen payments. In our sample schedule, reproduced earlier in this chapter, the amount is $1,133.63. Simple. Precise.

But what about the six days?

Mortgagors pay in advance. In other words, the fourteenth payment included the interest due for the entire fourteenth month. You owe him money. He has already paid interest for the use of your money throughout the fourteenth month, but will be using it for only six days. Take the interest portion of that monthly payment, $11.62, and reduce it to a daily interest rate. If the fourteenth month happens to be June, divide $11.62 by 30. The result is $.3873 per day. Your mortgagor is due an interest rebate for 24 days at $.3873 per day, or $9.30.

Of course, on the sixth day of the month, the fourteenth payment may not yet have been received. A delay is not uncommon when a mortgagor is anticipating completely repaying his loan.

Use the thirteenth line. Only thirteen payments have been received. Our sample schedule shows the loan balance to be $1,161.52.

The six days now represent money due you. Again, take the interest due for the fourteenth month, $11.62. Divide this by the number of days in the month in question. If it happens to be February, the result will be $11.62 divided by 28, or $.4168 per day. For the six days involved, the interest due would be $2.50

Accuracy

With so many tools available, there is absolutely no excuse for inaccuracy. As Chapter 11 clearly states, each jurisdiction imposes an interest limitation. Exceeding those limits invokes harsh penalties.

In a 9 per cent state, a four-year, two thousand dollar loan entitles the investor to $49.78 a month. Not $50.00, not $49.98. Forty-nine dollars and seventy-eight cents.

The same degree of accuracy is required in computing mortgage balances.

Use accurate aids. Be precise.

13

Preparing To Close A
Second Mortgage

Don't Be a Sitting Duck ... Wait for the Deed and Insurance
Policy ... Examining the Policy ... A Sample Policy ... The
Change Endorsement ... A Sample Change Endorsement ...
Mortgage Closing Check List ... Appraisal Form ... Preliminary
Attorney's Services ... Loan Closing Statements ... A Sample
Mortgage Note ... A Mortgage Deed ... Statement of Loan ...
Loan Amortization Schedule ... Final Coordination ... The Clos-
ing ... Some Loose Ends

Don't Be a Sitting Duck

We've come a long way since page one. Much information has
passed between us. Now, the theory of mortgage investment is about
to become a reality.

You have already completed the Initial Interview Form discussed
in detail in Chapter 8, and your borrower has completed your Loan
Application Form reprinted in that same chapter.

I must assume that you have carefully applied the Safety Formula
and the Ability-to-Pay Formula. Not to do so before your money
passes into the hands of the applicant is to transform an investment
into a speculation and an investor into a sitting duck.

Please, be cautious. Intuition has its place. At the races. Grocery
shopping. Treasure hunting.

But never, never, at the withdrawal window of the bank where you store your savings.

Be humble. Use the Safety Formula and the Ability-To-Pay Formula. Use the recommended forms. Save your impulse buying for less expensive pursuits.

Wait for the Deed and Insurance Policy

As I discussed earlier, regardless of how eager your applicant may appear, regardless of how agreeable he seems when you mention the monthly charges necessary to carry the mortgage he seeks, regardless of his apparent willingness to have you apply the mortgage proceeds directly to his debts, regardless of his insistence on concluding the transaction as quickly as possible, do nothing further until he confirms his interest by submitting his insurance policy and the deed to his home.

That's commitment. It takes effort to find that dusty old deed. A man really cares when he takes the effort to trudge to the corner mailbox or drive to your office.

Examining the Policy

Now. You have the insurance policy. What do you do with it?

First, check the names of the insured on the policy against the names of the property owners on the deed. If there is any discrepancy, the insurance policy should be changed to conform to the deed.

Check the address. If there is any discrepancy, the insurance policy should be changed to conform to the deed.

Check the dates. Most policies carry an inception and expiration date line just under the insured's name and address. Be certain the policy is still in effect, chronologically, at least.

Check the coverage. It should be enough to cover both the current balance of the first mortgage and the full amount of your second mortgage. If not, the coverage must be increased. Lack of adequate coverage means lack of adequate protection.

One item usually need not be checked. The first mortgage clause will rarely need changing. Except in the most extraordinary circumstances, the policy will list the name and address of the first mortgagee. (Unencumbered homes are rarely submitted to second mortgage in-

MEMORANDUM HOMEOWNERS POLICY

THE ÆTNA CASUALTY AND SURETY COMPANY
Hartford, Connecticut 06115, A Stock Insurance Company
THE STANDARD FIRE INSURANCE COMPANY
Hartford, Connecticut 06115, A Stock Insurance Company

☐ ☐

This memorandum of the policy as numbered below is for information only; it is not a contract of insurance but attests to the terms of the policy as of the date of its issuance. Said policy is subject to change by endorsement and to assignment and cancellation in accordance with its terms.

Policy Term	Policy Number
3 Years	07 HO 123456

Policy Period:
5/31/00 Inception — 5/31/00 Expiration
(Number, Street, Town, County, State)

Named Insured and Address (Number, Street, Town, County, State)

— John Doe & Helen Doe, ATSOT
— 901 Farmington Avenue
— West Hartford, Conn.
— Hartford County

The described premises covered hereunder are located at the above address, unless otherwise stated herein: (Number, Street, Town, County, State)

Insurance is provided only with respect to those of the following coverages which are indicated by a specific limit of liability applicable thereto.

Coverages	Limit of Liability
S A. Dwelling	$ 20,000.00
E B. Appurtenant Private Structures	$ 2,000.00
C C. Unscheduled Personal Property	$ 8,000.00
T D. Additional Living Expense	$ 4,000.00
I E. Personal Liability	$ 25,000 Each Occurrence
O (Bodily Injury and Property Damage)	
N F. Personal Medical Payments	$ 500 Each Person
II	$ 25,000 Each Accident
G. Physical Damage to Property of Others	$ 250 Each Occurrence

	Premium
Basic Policy Premium	$ 190.00
Additional Premium	$
Total Policy Premium	$ 190.00
Credit, if any, for existing insurance	$
Net Prepaid Premium	$ 190.00
Total Premium if paid in installments	$ 201.00
Payable:	
At Inception (and)	$ 67.00
At each subsequent anniversary	$ 67.00

Supplemental Personal Articles Floater Policy
$
$
$
$

SPECIMEN POLICY

Subject to the following Forms and Endorsements (Insert No. and Edition Date)
MIC-3(6/63); MIC-4(6/63); HO-60(6/64)

	Zone	Premium Group No.	Roof	construction is occupied by not more than two families and not more than two roomers or boarders per family.
The described dwelling of **frame**	II	14	☒ Approved ☐ Unapproved	

Protection Class	Not more than	Not more than
B	500 feet from Hydrant	3 miles from Fire Dept.

Applicable when only Form 4 is attached to this policy: Annual fire and extended coverage contents rate _____; number of apartments in building _____.

The described dwelling is not seasonal and no business pursuits are conducted at the premises thereof; Exceptions if any:

152

Figure 13-1.

| Business of Named Insured: | **Loss Deductible Clause No. 1**—Loss by windstorm or hail is **$50.00** applicable. |
| | **Loss Deductible Clause No. 2**—Loss by other perils is **$50.00** applicable. |

Special provisions applicable only in State(s) indicated:

| Southern States: South Carolina—Valuation Clause—$ | N.Y. Co-insurance Clause Applies: | N.Y. Fire District |
| ☐ Inside Protected Suburban Area ☐ Inside Fire District ☐ Inside City Limits | ☐ Yes ☐ No | |

Section II Only: (a) The described premises are the only premises where the Named Insured or spouse maintains a residence other than business property and farms; (b) Insured employs not more than two full-time residence employees; (c) The Insured owns no outboard motors of more than 24 horsepower for which coverage is desired. Exceptions, if any, to (a), (b) or (c): **no exceptions**

First Mortgagee: (Name and address)
Connecticut General Life Insurance Co., Cottage Grove Rd., Bloomfield, Conn.

Countersignature Date   Agency at **901 Farmington Ave.**
5/31/66   **West Hartford, Conn.   A.S. Haller**   A.S. AGENT

In Consideration of the Provisions and Stipulations Herein or Added Hereto and of the Premium Above Specified (or specified in endorsement attached hereto), the Stock Insurance Company indicated above by ☒, herein called "This Company," for the term **shown above** from **inception date shown above** (At Noon Standard Time) to **expiration date shown above** (At Noon Standard Time) at location of property involved, to an amount not exceeding the amount(s) above specified, does insure **the Insured named in the declarations above** and legal representatives, to the extent of the actual cash value of the property at the time of loss, but not exceeding the amount which it would cost to repair or replace the property with material of like kind and quality within a reasonable time after such loss, without allowance for any increased cost of repair or reconstruction by reason of any ordinance or law regulating construction or repair, and without compensation for loss resulting from interruption of business or manufacture, nor in any event for more than the interest of the Insured, against all DIRECT LOSS BY FIRE, LIGHTNING AND OTHER PERILS INSURED AGAINST IN THIS POLICY INCLUDING REMOVAL FROM PREMISES ENDANGERED BY THE PERILS INSURED AGAINST IN THIS POLICY, EXCEPT AS HEREINAFTER PROVIDED, to the property described herein while located or contained as described in this policy, or pro rata for five days at each proper place to which any of the property shall necessarily be removed for preservation from the perils insured against in this policy, but not elsewhere.

Assignment of this policy shall not be valid except with the written consent of this Company.

This policy is made and accepted subject to the foregoing provisions and stipulations and those hereinafter stated, which are hereby made a part of this policy, together with such other provisions, stipulations and agreements as may be added hereto, as provided in this policy.

153

vestors for short-term mortgage loans.) The policy should be amended to reflect your status as second mortgagee, however. This is so whether no second mortgagee is listed or whether your second mortgage is replacing a pre-existing second mortgage.

Such a listing assures you that money paid the insured in the event of loss by fire will be made available to you after the bank or insurance company serving as first mortgagee is covered.

It also assures you of advance notification of impending cancellation in the event your mortgagor neglects to pay his premiums.

A Sample Policy

The cover page of a specimen insurance policy is shown in Figure 13-1.

The Change Endorsement

We have reviewed five insurance items which you might wish to have changed: Name, address, effective date, coverage, and mortgage clause.

The mechanics of the change are simple. In all but the effective date and coverage items, call the agent directly and request a "change endorsement." He will be pleased to prepare and forward one by return mail.

Incidentally, the name, address, and telephone number of the insurance agent who wrote the policy will generally appear in the form of a sticker affixed to the upper right-hand corner of the first page of the policy or at the signature line towards the bottom of that page.

As regards coverage, call the applicant before calling his agent. Discuss the need for an increase and gain his permission to order the additional coverage. The cost will be small enough to stifle any protest. Certainly, the benefit of full protection should impress him, too. If the effective date has lapsed, the unprotected homeowner will be grateful for your astuteness.

When discussing any of these items with the broker, he will gladly advise you whether or not his assured has paid his premiums.

CHANGE and ATTACHING CLAUSE ENDORSEMENT

HO-135
(Ed. 9-62)

CFC ®

ttached to and forming part of:

olicy No. __07H0123456__ _____ of the __Aetna C&S__ _____

gency at __901 Farmington Ave., West Hartford, Conn.__ _____
                                              Name of Insurance Company

_____
City or Town   State

ffective Date
Endorsement __6/13/66__ ___ Date of Policy __5/31/66-5/31/69__ _____

lame of Insured __John Doe & Helen Doe, ATSOT__ _____

ocation __901 Farmington Ave., West Hartford, Conn.__ _____

A.S. Haller

_____ Agent

By _____

The policy is amended as follows:

Second Mortgagee is hereby added: John Wilson, 1655 Main Street, Hometown, Illinois

SPECIMEN ENDORSEMENT

PREMIUM RECAPITULATION

Due at Endorsement Effective Date:

	Additional Premium	Return Premium	
	$	$	

Premium adjustment if the Premium is payable in annual installments.

Dates Due	Original Installments	Increase	Decrease	Revised Installments
	$	$	$	$
	$	$	$	$
	$	$	$	$
	$	$	$	$
Total Premium to Policy Expiration	$	$		

ATTACH ENDORSEMENTS BELOW THIS LINE

Figure 13-2.

A Sample Change Endorsement

A specimen change endorsement form is shown in Figure 13-2.

Mortgage Closing Check List

Your next step is to use your Mortgage Closing Check List. Figure 13-2a.

Fill out the heading. If you have already chosen a closing date and time, fill them in. If not, you will be choosing one shortly.

The deed may supply the house number as well as the lot number, if any.

The owner's names should be precisely the same as appears on the applicant's deed.

In some cases, the Safety Formula will indicate borderline security. If the applicant is particularly appealing, well-employed, good income, good credit report, etc., he may be able to suggest an endorser or additional security. Sometimes such a possibility can tip the scales in his favor. If that situation exists, make note of it so that your attorney can prepare the appropriate documents.

The Check List is divided into two categories: work to be completed prior to the closing, and items to be attended to during the closing.

Let's concentrate on the "Prior" column first.

Order your credit report. Check the line under "Or'd" and note the name of the credit bureau, the date, and the member of the bureau from whom the report was ordered. Be certain to establish the date upon which you can expect to receive the report. Note that, too.

Appraisal Form

Next, unless you have made other arrangements, discussed at

MORTGAGE CLOSING CHECK LIST

Closing Date _____ Time _____

Property _____ _____   _____
      House No.   Lot No.   Street

    _____   _____
      Town   County

Owners _____

Endorser _____

Other Security _____

	Or'd	Rec'd		Checked	Cmpltd.
PRIOR:			**CLOSING:**		
Credit Check	___	___	Mortgage Deed	___	___
by					
credit appr'd by	___	___			
			Mortgage Note	___	___
Appraisal	___	___	sign by		
by	$				
by	$		Insurance Change	___	___
Exist. Mtg.	$		mtgor.		
			address		
Insur. Change Endorse.	___	___	dates		
from			amount		
			2nd mtgee.		
Search	___	___	signed		
by					
			Adjustment Sheet	___	___
Amortiza. Sched.	___	___			
Draft:			Pay Debts	___	___
Mortgage Deed	___	___			
Late chg.	___	___	Cost of Recordg.Rel.	___	___
Mortgage Note	___	___			
$____ , ____yrs.			Other		
$____ monthly					
Adjustment Sheet	___	___			
mortgage			**POST CLOSING:**		
interest					
legal services			Certificate of Title	___	___
recording			Amort. Sched. to Mtgr.	___	___
pay off debts:			Interest to Investor	___	___
			Deduct Amort. Sched.	___	___
balance:			Paid Broker's Commission	___	___
Other:					

Figure 13-2a.

length in Chapter 9, call your appraiser. Where appropriate, send him a copy of your Appraisal Form for completion. (See Figure 13-3.) Because his task can only be accomplished by invading the private domain of your applicant and examining his home, it is wise for you to prepare for his inquisitive visit by discussing it with the applicant and assuring him that the appraiser will call for an appointment. Any unpleasantness occasioned by his visit can only corrode the relationship you are seeking to create. The intrusion will be less traumatic if it is anticipated. Women, particularly, feel much better when they have an opportunity to "straighten up."

APPRAISAL FORM

Name   Address   Town

Type of neighborhood: Trend of area:

Comparison with neighboring homes:

Style: Families   Year built   Lot Size

Usable living area:

Construction	Interior walls	No. rooms
Baths	Full basement	Plumbing
Heating & fuel	Fireplaces	Floors
Roof	Porches	Garages
Combination storms	Electricity	Gas
Sidewalks	Curbs	Sewers or septic
Street	Neighborhood	Shopping
Bus line	Taxes	

Comparable sales:

Appraiser's evaluation

Figure 13-3.

Preliminary Attorney's Services

Call your attorney. Advise him that you plan to place a second mortgage and wish to be assured that the bank's mortgage is the only lien on the property. After all, if a $20,000 home has a $10,000 mortgage, your $1,500 second mortgage is fine — unless there is a tax lien, an attachment and a sewer caveat ahead of you. In any event, your attorney will supply a Certificate of Title or Title Insurance Policy setting forth the precise status of the title to the property.

Ask him to prepare a mortgage deed, a note, and loan closing statement.

In order to provide your attorney with the necessary details, tell him:

(a) The amount of the mortgage loan.
(b) The term of the mortgage.
(c) The interest rate.
(d) The monthly payments.
(e) The date the first full monthly payment will be due.
(f) The amount and name of each creditor to be paid from the mortgage proceeds.

Interest payments will be either known to the attorney or computable by him after reference to items (a), the amount of the mortgage loan; (b), the interest rate; and (c), the date of first full monthly payment.

Now the attorney can proceed to create the Loan Closing Statement, sometimes known as the Adjustment Sheet. See the closing check list, towards the bottom of the "Prior" column. He tabulates the advance interest payment, the fee for legal services, the cost of recording, and the amount (if any) to be applied to paying existing debts. The remaining figure represents the full mortgage loan balance.

Loan Closing Statements

As a guide, I have created a typical simple Loan Closing Statement, itemizing the disbursement of all the mortgage funds.

The statement is dated and prepared in duplicate, one for each party.

LOAN CLOSING STATEMENT

Re: 123 Typical Street
San Francisco, California

Mortgage		$2,000.00
Interest		
January 18-31 at $.6451 per diem	9.03	
Attorney's Fees	85.00	
Recording Fees	9.00	
Balance to mortgagors	1,896.97	
	$2,000.00	$2,000.00

January 18, 19--.

_____

Andrew Mortgagor

_____

Alice Mortgagor

_____

Marvin Mortgagee

First monthly payment: February 1, 19--.

Figure 13-4.

This is a simple Loan Closing Statement, one providing for the payment of interest due for the balance of the month and the transfer to the mortgagors of all the mortgage proceeds.

A more complex statement is shown in Figure 13-5.

LOAN CLOSING STATEMENT

Re: 123 Typical Street
San Francisco, California

Mortgage		$2,000.00
Interest		
January 18-31 at $.6451 per diem	$ 9.03	
February	20.00	
Attorney's fees	85.00	
Recording fees	9.00	
Local Bank and Trust Co.	200.00	
Men's Shop, Inc.	114.69	
Nearby Finance Company	317.14	
Another Bank and Trust Co.	197.42	
Electric Company	62.21	
Corner Grocery Store	47.38	
The Department Store	423.57	
Family Doctor	135.73	
Local Oil Company	126.41	
Balance to Mortgagors	252.42	
	$2,000.00	$2,000.00

January 18, 19--.

_____
Andrew Mortgagor

_____
Alice Mortgagor

_____
Marvin Mortgagee

First monthly payment March 1, 19--.

Figure 13-5.

The Figure 13-5 includes two refinements. Not only is the interest charged to the last day of the month of the closing, as in the first sample, but also included is interest due for the subsequent month. As a result, the first regular monthly payment is postponed to the following month, March first, instead of the first day of February. This serves to give a harried debtor a breather as well as earn the mortgagee additional interest.

The Figure 13-5 also illustrates the manner in which mortgage funds are used when the purpose of the loan is consolidation of debts. After confirming the money due with each creditor, every creditor's check is marked, "Payment in full to date on the account of Andrew and Alice Mortgagor," and mailed by the attorney.

A Sample Mortgage Note

I do not for a moment suggest that your attorney is in need of assistance in drafting a mortgage note. I certainly cannot suggest that I am aware of the nuances of mortgage law in other than my own jurisdiction.

It may prove to be of some value, nevertheless, to reproduce the mortgage note currently used by my office in second mortgage transactions. It contains phrases that have evolved over the years to meet patterns that rose to plague mortgage holders. (See Figure 13-6).

Notice that there is no use of the euphemism, "One per cent a month" on the original balance. It's a   12   per cent mortgage, and that's what it's called.

The default period (see Item No.1) is shorter than many. This is a judgment to be made independently in view of all the local circumstances.

The mortgagor is not permitted to transfer his home, with this second mortgage intact, to another homeowner. To permit him to do so would be to permit him to choose a complete stranger as your mortgagor, someone who may be totally unable to meet your Ability-to-Pay standards (Item No. 2).

No additional mortgages, either. Why should you stand by while the mortgagor commits fiscal suicide? (Item No. 3)

He must keep his first mortgage payments current. With each payment that is made, your Safety Formula percentage looks better

SAMPLE MORTGAGE NOTE

$ Connecticut

                                                                19

FOR VALUE RECEIVED, the undersigned, jointly and severally,
promise(s) to pay to   , or order,
the principal sum of
($), with interest from date at the rate of
                   per cent (%) per annum on the unpaid
balance until paid. The said principal and interest shall be
payable at the office of
                                      , or at such other place
as the holder may designate in writing, in monthly installments
of   ($),
commencing on the first day of   , 19   ,
and on the first day of each month thereafter until the principal
and interest are fully paid, except that the final payment of
principal and interest, if not sooner paid, shall be due and
payable on the first day of   , 19

    Each payment shall be applied by the holder: first, to
interest on the unpaid principal balance, and second, to the
unpaid principal balance.

    The whole of this note shall be rendered immediately due
and payable at the option of the holder hereof, without necessity
for demand and notice, under any one of the following circumstances:

1.   Default, for a period of ten days after any of the same
   shall become due and payable, in the payment of any of said
   mortgage installments, or in taxes, municipal assessments,
   or fire insurance premiums on the premises mortgages to
   secure this note, or of taxes on this note.
2.   Vesting of the title to said property in anyone other than
   the undersigned.
3.   Permitting the premises to be additionally encumbered in
   any manner whatsoever.
4.   Default in the performance of any of the agreements or provisions in the mortgage deed securing this note.
5.   Default in the payments of any obligation secured by any
   other mortgage on subject premises.
6.   Failure to keep said premises insured for the benefit and
   to the satisfaction of the holder of this note.

I or We agree to pay all costs of collection, including reasonable attorney's fees incurred in protecting or sustaining the lien of the mortgage securing this note, or incurred after default in any condition of this note or in said mortgage to collect this note or foreclose said mortgage.

Privilege is given the maker hereof after a total of monthly payments of principal and interest have been made, (1) to repay the entire unpaid principal sum of this note, plus interest to the date of payment, at any time; (2) to pay on the principal, on any day on which a principal payment is due, an amount equal to one or more of the principal payments next due.

This note is secured by mortgage or even date herewith on property located at

_____ L.S.

_____ L.S.

Figure 13-6.

and better. When he begins to skip that first mortgage, though, even while promptly paying yours, it's just a matter of time before the water starts to bubble. (Item No. 4)

Our policy is to permit mortgagors to prepay without penalty providing we are assured a minimum amount of interest. After all, the loan has involved considerable energy and expense. At the present, the guaranteed interest is for two years. It had been one year for a long while. The choice is yours.

A Mortgage Deed

The deed is a simple printed form. Each jurisdiction has legal stationers who supply them at low cost. The major item of interest, perhaps, is the special stamp I have had made. It is applied to the most conspicuous space in the form, and reads:

NONTRANSFERABLE MORTGAGE

Yes, the note clearly advises anyone who reads it that it becomes immediately due and payable upon the transfer of the premises. There is just no point in permitting any misunderstanding.

The stamp, in one word, clears the air beautifully.

Statement Of Loan

Prepare your Statement of Loan. I've discussed this earlier (Chapter 8).

The Statement of Loan is a simple document, but one calculated to remove all possible confusion in the mind of the borrower.

A sample Statement is reprinted for your examination.

As you can see, the upper portion carries the major statutory enactments controlling loans in the State of Connecticut. It advises the borrower of his rights.

The excerpts are not complete, but they do cover the high spots. And they certainly tell the average borrower more than he has ever known before.

When this form was first created, a copy was forwarded to the local Better Business Bureau. The manager was enthusiastic, so enthusiastic that he reprinted the statutory outline in the next issue of the *Better Business News of Greater Hartford.*

The bottom portion advises the borrower in easily understood statistics the precise terms of his loan, the true annual interest rate, and the total amount he will repay.

How many institutions do you know that are honest enough to present such a statement to their customers?

The Loan Statement should be prepared in duplicate. Sign one for the borrowers. Have them sign one for you.

Don't bother to type them anew for each mortgage. Either mimeograph a number of them, or photostat sets from a master as you need them. Then just fill in the blanks.

It's a good, clean way of doing business.

STATEMENT OF LOAN

CONNECTICUT GENERAL STATUTES

Section 37-4 Loans at greater rate than twelve percent prohibited.

Section 37-5 No person and no firm or corporation . . . shall, with intent to evade the provisions of Section 37-4, accept a note or notes for a greater amount than actually loaned.

Section 37-6 No person shall charge a borrower with any expense of inquiry as to his financial responsibility or expense of negotiating a loan, or charge at the time of making a loan, the expense of collecting the interest and principal of the loan, unless the total of such charges and of the interest agreed upon is, during any one year, 12 percent of the loan or less.

Section 37-9 The provisions of Sections 37-4, 37-5 and 37-6 shall not effect any . . . bona fide mortgage of real property for a sum in excess of five thousand dollars . . . For the purpose of this Section, "interest" shall not be construed to include attorney's fees including preparation of mortgage deed and note, title search, waivers and closing fees or recording fees paid by the mortgagor.

Dear

The paragraphs reprinted are some of the laws of the State of Connecticut regarding legal interest rates and charges for loans and mortgages.

We are lending you $ in cash for   months.

You will repay $, at   % per month on the unpaid balance, or total of   % a year.

The total amount you will repay will be $

Your true annual interest rate for the life of the loan is approximately   %.

_____

_____

_____

Loan Amortization Schedule

Order a duplicate set of the appropriate loan amortization schedule. We discussed those loan reduction statements in detail in Chapter 12.

Because they eliminate periodic telephone calls asking for the balance of the mortgage, they are well worth the price. Two for one dollar.

They also eliminate a telephone call two o'clock in the morning just before the mortgagor's income tax is due, asking how much was paid towards interest last year.

Perhaps their greatest value is that they are readily accepted as the impartial authority. When each party has a schedule, there's just no question about the balance of the loan.

Final Coordination

Now your office, or your home, if you transact your mortgage loan business from your home, becomes a communications center. You become a coordinator.

All the necessary items have been ordered.

Mortgage Note — your attorney

Mortgage Deed — your attorney

Loan Closing Statement — your attorney

Certificate of Title — your attorney

Credit Report — your credit bureau

Amortization Schedule — your financial publishing house

Insurance Policy Change Endorsement — your mortgagor's insurance agent

Appraisal — your appraiser

Statement of Loan — you or your attorney.

When they arrive, you are ready to close. As a matter of fact, you can close the mortgage before the Amortization Schedule arrives. It is not a necessary part of the closing ceremonies, and its late arrival provides a fine excuse to enclose a short, friendly note reminding the mortgagor the date, amount, and mailing address of his first payment.

If you operate from a checking account, you might have the checks prepared in advance to facilitate the disbursement of funds.

First, draw a check payable to both mortgagors in the full amount of the loan. Endorse the reverse side, "Pay to the order of (your name or your attorney's)."

Then either you or your attorney will prepare the checks disbursing the mortgage loan.

One, to the official who will record the documents.

Another, to your attorney for his services.

Another, to yourself for interest due prior to the first full payment.

Others, as many as are necessary, to pay the debts agreed upon between yourself and the mortgagor.

Finally, the balance available to the mortgagor.

Conduct the transaction at your attorney's office. The atmosphere is a good one. It is professional, austere, and somewhat somber.

In addition, the attorney is your friend, and an old pro. If anything unusual arises, he will know how to handle it.

Before passing papers to the mortgagors, your attorney will be certain that the names on the documents, the descriptions, the credit report, the change endorsement, the appraisal, and the preliminary certificate of title, are all on hand, in proper form, and have been cross-checked to insure accuracy.

The Closing Check List will be a good guide.

The Closing

The order I recommend is as follows:

1. Review the note aloud with the mortgagors. Amount. Monthly payments. Number of payments. Make particular note of date first payment is due. Discuss the grace period before a late charge, if any, or mortgage default, may be declared. Carefully discuss prepayment privileges.

Mortgagors sign.

Original to investor.

Copy to mortgagors.

2. Review mortgage deed.

Mortgagors sign. Witnesses. Acknowledgment.

Original to investor.

Copy to mortgagors.

3. Read Loan Settlement Statement.

Use a scratch pad to explain in detail why the balance to the mortgagors is an accurate figure. People just do not seem to catch on the first time around. They act as if they do, smiling weakly through bewildered eyes. Do everyone a favor and use the scratch pad. Three times, if necessary.

Investor signs.

Mortgagors sign.

Original to investor.

Copy to mortgagor.

4. If it has arrived, pass a copy of the Amortization Schedule to the mortgagors. Take a moment to illustrate how it is used to find the mortgage balance, and put a light pencil line around the tax deductable interest payments.

5. Read the Statement of Loan. Any questions?

Investor signs mortgagor's copy.

Mortgagors sign investor's copy.

6. Show the check representing the mortgage loan amount to the mortgagors. Turn it over to the restrictive endorsement and ask them to sign. The restrictive endorsement should read, "Pay to the Order of (whoever will be making out the disbursement checks)."

7. You or your attorney sign the disbursement checks, totalling the amount of the mortgage loan, and distribute them.

The closing is over.

Some Loose Ends

If you have obligated yourself to pay a commission to a mortgage broker or a realtor, now's the time to do it. Don't delay. It corrodes your agent's eagerness to continue the relationship.

Pay all your bills immediately.

Your attorney's check has already been drawn. It was one of the items on the Loan Settlement Statement. Pass it across the table to him now. If he is the one who will record the mortgage deed, pass him the recording cost check as well.

You have an appraisal fee, a credit report charge, and the cost of the amortization schedule to meet.

Make your payments the day your bills arrive.

At the conclusion of the closing, make it a point to write out your name and address, the amount of the monthly payment, and the date the first payment is due. Don't prepare that memo in advance. Do it while your mortgagors are watching. Ask, "Who pays the bill?" Say, "Well, then, this is for you" — and write the memo while he watches. It will help his memory.

Then discuss the psychology of prompt payments. And stress the value to the mortgagor of maintaining a pattern of prompt payments. But the details of this discussion will have to wait until Chapter 15.

Be certain to record your mortgage deed in the appropriate land record office.

14

Managing Your Mortgages

Safeguarding Valuables ... Creating a Mortgage File ... A Transmittal Letter ... Insurance Default ... Creating an Account Book ... Handling the Monthly Checks ... Posting the Safety Formula ... Follow the Bouncing Ball ... An Investment Group — Monthly Earnings ... An Investment Group — Distribution of Profits

Safeguarding Valuables

You are now in possession of some rather valuable documents: mortgage note, mortgage deed (after it has been recorded in the land record office and returned), insurance policy, Change Endorsement, and Certificate of Title or title insurance policy.

You have also accumulated some interesting items worthy of being maintained: Initial Interview Form, Loan Application, Appraisal, Closing Check List, Loan Settlement Statement, Statement of Loan, and Amortization Schedule.

The first group, the valuable group, belongs in a secure place: a safe, a safety deposit box, or a fire-proof file cabinet with lock.

Creating a Mortgage File

The second group should be maintained together in a separate file for each mortgage.

Perforate each item to be placed in the file with a punch that will center two holes approximately three inches apart at the top of each sheet.

Perforate the right-hand side of your file folder in the same manner.

Pass the arms of a soft metal fastener through the holes from the file folder forward through the papers, and then spread the arms of the metal fastener to hold the papers in place.

Place one sheet of blank paper on top. Then as each check is received, record the date of the check, the date received, the amount, and the number of the check. See Figure 14-1.

MORTGAGOR, JOHN AND IRENE

CHECK DATED	CHECK RECEIVED	AMOUNT	CHECK NUMBER
May 1	May 8	$44.49	237
May 30	June 1	44.49	244
July 1	July 2	44.49	251
August 3	August 4	44.49	256

Figure 14-1.

Should you be that member of an investment group charged with the responsibility of collecting payments and passing them on to the Treasurer for deposit to the group's account, you have one further step to take.

A Transmittal Letter

Create a cover letter, or a letter of transmittal, for each check, a simple letter, mimeographed in advance, but sufficient to evidence each check transmitted.

Such a letter would be addressed to the group's treasurer and read initially as follows:

Re: Capitol City Investments —
Dear Dave:

I have enclosed a check in the amount of $ being the payment in the above-captioned mortgage to Capitol City Investments.

Very truly,

You need do only four simple things:
1. Date the letter.
2. Fill in the last name of the mortgagor on the Re: line after "Capitol City Investment."
3. Fill in the amount of the payment being forwarded.
4. Sign the letter.

Thus, your completed form letter created in duplicate would read as follows:

August 4

Re: Capitol City Investments — Andrew Mortgagor

Dear Dave:

I have enclosed a check in the amount of $44.49, being the payment in the above-captioned mortgage to Capitol City Investments.

Very truly,

Marvin Mortgagee

Keep the duplicate copy on the left-hand side of your file, perforated and secured in the same manner as the other papers.

Now, your file is complete.

Assuming your attorney has properly recorded the mortgage deed, your task, with this mortgage, is limited to administering the monthly checks and encouraging prompt payment. The mortgage deed, incidentally, will be returned to you by the recording official after a true copy has been incorporated into the real estate records.

Insurance Default

It is possible for the mortgagor to default in his insurance payments, thus depriving your investment of protection against the destruction of your security. Your position is improved, however, when you receive a Change Endorsement naming you the second mortgagee.

Should a default be imminent, the insurance carrier will notify you well in advance.

You will then have the choice of discussing the problem with your mortgagor and convincing him to meet his premium payments now and in the future, or exercising Clause No. 6 of your mortgage note reading:

> The whole of this note shall be rendered immediately due and payable . . . under any one of the following circumstances:
> 6. Failure to keep said premises insured for the benefit and to the satisfaction of the holder of this note.

Creating an Account Book

Maintain an account book to facilitate following the progress of your mortgage portfolio at a glance.

The preferable style is a spiral binder twelve-column book. See Figure 14-2.

YEAR _____			JAN.	FEB.	MAR.	APRIL	MAY	JUN
1. Jones	$1500/3	$49.83	1/3	2/2	3/2	5/2	6/6	7/2
2. Smith	2000/4	52.67	1/2	2/3	3/2	5/3	6/2	7/3
3. Brown	1500/4	39.51	1/5	2/4	3/3	5/2	6/3	7/2
4. Phillips	1500/5	33.37	1/2	2/2	3/2	5/2	6/3	7/3

Figure 14-2.

Skip the first page and open it to the second page, creating a double page. Generally, one-half of the left-hand page will have space for all the information you might wish to list: the number of the mortgage, the last name of the mortgagor, the amount of the mortgage, and the term, and the monthly payment.

There will then be four columns to the right of the spaces, and eight columns on the right-hand page. Label each column, with a month, label the pages with the year — presto — you are ready.

Now, as each check arrives, in addition to the four entries that you make on the cover sheet of the individual mortgage file, post the date of receipt of each payment under the month the payment is due. If your first payment is due in November, whether the check is received in October, November, or December, list the date of receipt under the November column.

The account book is the source of other information, too.

I recommend maintaining a penciled total figure under the monthly payment column to enable you to see the total amount of income expected monthly.

As the months and years pass, some mortgages will be paid off in advance, or may be rewritten to the original, or a slightly higher, amount. See Figure 14-3.

YEAR _____			JAN.	FEB.	MAR.	APR.	MAY	JUNE
1 Jones	$1500/3	$49.83	1/3	2/2	3/2	4/2		
2 Smith	2000/4	52.67	1/2	2/3	3/2	paid off	APR. 4/66	
3 Brown	1500/4	39.57	1/4	1/31	3/3			
4 Phillips	1500/5	33.37	1/2	2/2	3/2	re-written	APR. 11/66	
		175.38						
5 Phillips	2000/5	44.49						
		133.83						

Figure 14-3.

Any mortgage paid in full or rewritten is removed from the rolls by running a fine red line through it and noting the action taken and the date.

If the note is to be rewritten, a new listing will be entered and the new information inscribed. This applies even when the mortgage is rewritten for the original amount under identical terms. New amount or old, the original mortgage is released and a totally new mortgage is initiated.

It would be well to check the box representing the month the first payment is due to save you the inconvenience of referring to the individual file of a new mortgagor when the first of the month rolls around.

Handling the Monthly Checks

As for the monthly checks, there are two steps that should be followed.

The first is a time saver. The second is a technique for assuring accuracy.

After you have written a number of mortgages, it would be wise to order a rubber stamp to eliminate the bother of manual endorsement of each check — and, incidentally, to insure the accuracy of each endorsement.

The bank with whom you maintain your mortgage checking account will be pleased to order this stamp for you, and generally will absorb the cost.

When making deposits to your account, I suggest preparing duplicate deposit slips. The carbon copy is for your file. The original will be retained by the bank. Each will be identically stamped by the teller.

The advantage of retaining a bank-stamped carbon copy of the deposit slip is radically increased when you take the time to note the name of each mortgagor alongside his check's transit number.

		Dollars	Cents
Deposit Ticket			
	Bills		
Date _____			
	Coins		
	Checks 51-44 Jones	49	83
	51-57 Brown	39	51
Bank & Trust Co.	51-57 Philips	44	49
Detroit, Michigan	Total	133	83

You now have a fine source from which to reconstruct any set of facts bearing on the status of your accounts.

Posting the Safety Formula

At this point it is appropriate to find your Safety Formula computation and place it at the upper left-hand corner of the front cover of the file.

Do it in clear, bold strokes.

Your Safety Formulas will look like this:

$$67\% \,+\, 3,300, \text{ or}$$
$$72\% \,+\, 3,200 \text{ or}$$
$$64\% \,+\, 5,100.$$

Let's review the meaning. A home appraises for $10,000 and carries a $5,200 first mortgage and your $1,500 second mortage.

$5,200
+1,500
$6,700

$$\begin{array}{r} .67 = 67\% \\ 10,000 \overline{\smash{)}\ 6,700.00} \\ \underline{6,000\ 0} \\ 700\ 00 \\ \underline{700\ 00} \end{array}$$

10,000
-6,700
$3,300   + $3,300

The shorthand formula reads 67 per cent + $3,300. What we are really saying is that the total of the first and second mortgages equals only 67 per cent of the conservativly appraised value of the property — and, further, a safety margin of $3,300 exists between the mortgage totals and the conservativly appraised value.

Placing the Safety Formula right smack on the top of the front cover of each mortgage file has many advantages.

Some day your sympathy may overcome your business acumen. You may agree to write a thin mortgage, a poor risk. Your $1,500 loan might have an 86 per cent Safety Formula rating and a $1,400 margin. If your experience is typical, it's the poor Safety Formula loans that will cause you sleepless nights. Every time a late payment comes in, a check bounces, or an insurance premium is left unpaid, you will reach for the file.

That Safety Formula will be right there, staring you in the face! After a while, you'll get so that you can't bear to see a high percentage, or a low margin, on a file. And that's good!

Keeping the Safety Formula out front is a good sales technique, too. Chapters 18 and 20 will discuss that in detail.

Follow the Bouncing Ball

One irritant that occurs with some regularity, and gnashing of teeth, is the bouncing check.

Don't get upset. It's just one of those things.

Just shrug your shoulders and call your mortgagor's bank. Explain that his depositor had given you a check in the amount of $33.37 that was returned for insufficient funds. Are there sufficient funds in the account now to cover the check?

Chances are, the money will be there. If not today, probably tomorrow. If not tomorrow, call your mortgagor and let him handle the problem.

Should this occasional bad check become a personal parade, stop shrugging your shoulders. Square them and get tough. No more personal checks. Money orders or certified checks, only. Period. Transfer the inconvenience to the knuckle-head who started it all.

An Investment Group — Monthly Earnings

Administration becomes complex only when servicing an investment group — and even then, the complexities can be mastered by the use of some basic mathematical skills.

Assume twenty-four members. Assume a varying investment pattern. Some members invest $25 a month, others $50, a few $75, and the balance invest $100 a month. That's about as tough a situation as you are likely to find.

How do you assign earnings?

It's simple, really. As you will recall from the sample Partnership Agreement outlined in Chapter 7, Section 24(a) directs, "Profits shall be allocated monthly towards Fund shares outstanding at the end of the preceding month."

Let's assume it's March and you now know that your group earned $346.72 during February. Those earnings will be divided among the number of shares outstanding at the end of January. Total them. If there were 588 shares purchased as of that date, divide $346.72 by 588 shares.

$$
\begin{array}{r}
\$\quad.59 \\
588\ \overline{)\$346.92} \\
294\ 0 \\
\hline
52\ 92 \\
52\ 92 \\
\hline
\end{array}
$$

Voila! Each January share earned $.59. Let's see. In January, Syd had sixteen shares. That's $9.44 for him. Dan had twenty-two shares. He earned $12.98. And so on down the list. Sure, it's tedious. But it's not really difficult.

To take this one step further, let's assume it's now April. Earnings are up to $401.14 for the month of March. We tabulate the number of shares outstanding during February. The total is 647.

$$
\begin{array}{r}
\$\quad.62 \\
647\ \overline{)\$401.14} \\
388\ 2 \\ \hline
12\ 94 \\
12\ 94 \\ \hline
\end{array}
$$

Each February share earned $.62. Syd had 18 shares in February and Dan had twenty-five. Thus, they earned $11.16 and $15.50, respectively.

An Investment Group — Distribution of Profits

If you elect to follow the form of the sample Partnership Agreement, at the end of the year you merely total each member's monthly earnings.

"24(b) Profits shall be distributed at the Annual Meeting in the form of shares in the Fund."

Assuming that your shares have a value of twenty-five dollars, if Syd earned a total of $152.52 for January through December, he would receive six additional shares at the annual meeting, and a credit of $2.52 towards the purchase of his next share.

15

Encouraging Prompt Payments

Educating Mortgagors ... Weed Out Improbables ... An Open
Line of Credit ... Correcting a Mistake ... Opportunity Knocks
at Least Twice ... Recommend Courtesy ... Don't Just Stand
There. Jump ... Three Times Is Too Much ... No Is the Best
Policy ... Don't Expect Perfection ... Phil and Ralph ... Looks
Like a Blue Chip ... Becoming a Partner

Educating Mortgagors

The money that will flow steadily into your mail box each month
will be a source of initial amazement and eventual deep satisfaction.
As long as it flows, that is.

Having followed the policies and principals of choosing mortgagor
with whom it would be safe to invest, you now face a new — and
equally vital — policy. You must educate your mortgagors to make
prompt payments.

Never, never forget that you are an investor, not a bill collector.
There isn't a reason in the world why you should undertake the tedious
task of pursuing your mortgagors every thirty days, pleading for your
payment.

If you do, the fault is yours. Your mortgagors, as is the case with
most people, will generally do whatever is expected of them. If you
gloss over the importance of prompt payments, so will they.

If you make an issue of the enormous importance you place on prompt payment, you will find that your borrowers will respect your wishes and meet the standards you have set.

The question, of course, is how do you discipline adults without arousing their ire? How do you lecture them, prod them, or brainwash them, without losing them?

It's simple, really.

Be honest with them. They want to please, and will not resent your discussing what you will expect of them in the months to come, providing you make your standards known early in the game, while they still have a chance to bow out.

Being honest eliminates any possibility of misunderstanding, and enables the mortgagor to set his course of conduct with confidence, secure that he is doing the right thing.

Weed Out Improbables

Scrupulous adherence to the Ability-to-Pay Formula will eliminate those who will fall behind because they have undertaken too heavy a series of loan payments.

You will inevitably meet a debtor harnessed with $190 a month in loan payments. He's hopeless. He cannot possibly meet those bills on his $95 a week income. When he approaches you for a second mortgage to pay off the oppressive loans, you quickly point out that his first and second mortgage payments would then total $137 a month.

"So what?" he asks. "If I could carry the $190 a month, I can certainly carry $137."

Nuts. He never "carried" $190. He collapsed under the weight. Those payments threw him into a tailspin and changed his wife into a bill-collector avoiding recluse.

Sure, $137 a month is better. It will buy him some time. But inevitably he will collapse under the weight once more. It will just take a bit longer this time.

Be brutally frank during your first interview, whether it be on the telephone or in person.

An Open Line of Credit

Tell your borrower that, if he develops a good history of prompt payments as the years pass, you will stand ready, at a moment's notice, to renew the loan back to its original amount, or perhaps a bit higher. If his payments are right on the button, he has opened a new line of instant credit. He will have the money the same day he calls, if necessary.

Now, don't underestimate the importance of an open line of credit to some one who is borrowing money to pay bills. His credit rating has probably suffered. He wants to get back to good standing.

Suddenly, you are a source of more than just an initial flow of money. You are a potential source of repeated money as well as a new credit rating.

Capitalize on this. Remind him that whenever he applies for a loan in the future, you will be called by the credit rating bureau for your experience with him.

An enthusiastic response will do wonders for the mortgagor. A negative reply — that his payments are always late, or that his checks bounce — will dig his hole even deeper.

The key to the value of this approach is that you are simply informing your mortgagor of his new circumstances. You are telling him the truth. Many borrowers never quite understand how their credit rating can be affected by a loan of this sort. Many borrowers never quite understand what course of conduct will best serve them in their relationship with their mortgagee.

By being completely candid, you are performing a service. To each of you.

Conclude with the statement that, while he will enjoy dealing with you as long as his payments arrive on time, and that being able to borrow additional cash by renewing his mortgage is a valuable asset, you are rather harsh with people who make late payments.

Tell him frankly that you are not a professional mortgage investor. You do it during your spare time and haven't the patience, the time, or the organization to chase poor payers. If he falls behind, you will have to ask him to pay off the loan in full and go somewhere else.

This, too, is nothing more than a candid insight into the mode of your operation.

Correcting a Mistake

If one of your mortgages causes you trouble, I strongly advise you to unload it.

Happily, unloading the loan need not be difficult.

There are quite a few second mortgage investors around. No, that's not quite true. There are quite a few men in every community who lend money, using second mortgages as their security. Most of them are not investors. They are gamblers.

Why? Simply because they never analyze their mortgage balances in relation to the appraised value of the mortgage property and draw the line at a conservative 70 per cent average. If they were investors, they would use our Safety Formula.

At any rate, even your bad mortgages will be vastly superior to the loans they hold. Selling them should be easy. Often the mortgagor himself will be able to find a new loan.

There it is. Your first conference. You've told him what you expect of him if he qualifies, what benefits he will receive if he behaves himself, and what the penalty will be if he does not meet his obligations.

At that point, ask him directly, "Do you feel you will be able to pay this promptly every month? Can you establish the habit of mailing your check a day or two before the first of each month?"

Wait for his reply. His response to your challenge is important.

Opportunity Knocks at Least Twice

Chances are, this first interview will be with just one of the two homeowners. If this is so, take full advantage of the circumstances when you meet the co-owner. Tell her that you have discussed the payment schedule with her husband. Repeat your conversation.

Conclude by telling her that it would be a shame for them to become obligated for a monthly series of payments if their habits are such that the payments will be late. Late payments will not be tolerated. What does she think?

Wait for her reply.

At the closing itself, repeat your approach once again.

Something along the line of: "Now, you know how I feel about late payments. Please develop the habit of mailing your checks on the thirtieth of every month. You'll never regret it. Do that regularly and I'll always be available to help you if you run into any trouble."

They'll get the message.

Recommend Courtesy

One further point. Stress the fact that if they are going to be late, they should courteously call or write to tell you to expect a late payment. If they merely ignore the payment date, you can't help but be annoyed. On the other hand, if they are concerned enough, and considerate enough, to contact you, you can't help but be more sympathetic.

This would be particularly so if they had established a prompt payment pattern with their earlier payments.

And there is another advantage of creating a pattern of timely monthly payments. After an extended string of payments arriving on the 31st or first, you will certainly cooperate when your mortgagor calls to explain that her husband has been out of work for two weeks and they will not be able to scrape the payment together until the twentieth.

Don't Just Stand There. Jump

Make certain to call or write immediately when the last mail delivery of the first day of the month passes without a check.

Jump on them.

June first

Dear Mr. and Mrs. Jones:

I was surprised to find that your mortgage payment was not in today's mail.

Perhaps the date slipped your mind.

Please forward the check immediately. I would suggest that you mail your next check on June 30th.

Very truly,

The letter is concise and to the point. It is pleasant, but firm. If no reply is received by return mail, become a bit more aggressive.

June fourth

Dear Mr. and Mrs. Jones:

When you borrowed my money, you promised to pay promptly.

You agreed to mail your check so that I would receive it on the first of the month.

Today is the fourth of June. Your payment is late.

I expect to receive your check immediately and to receive all future checks on time.

Very truly,

Three Times Is Too Much

The final letter will rarely be necessary. If it is, give serious thought to eliminating the mortgage. Have the borrower find a new loan and pay yours in full.

If you have to follow the full routine for two consecutive months, don't think about it — just close out the loan. Tell the mortgagor that you will not permit him to remain as a borrower. If he can't find someone to write a new mortgage, you find the new mortgagee for him.

The last letter should be forwarded by certified mail, return receipt requested, and read:

June eleventh

Dear Mr. and Mrs. Jones:

Your mortgage is now in default.

The entire balance of the loan is due, and I demand payment in full.

If you do not have the cash available, I suggest that you immediately find a new borrower and write a new mortgage large enough to pay me the full balance due.

Unless you do so immediately, it will be necessary for me to refer your mortgage to my attorney for foreclosure.

Very Truly,

Never make idle threats. If you say you will refer the mortgage to your attorney for foreclosure, do it. Do it promptly. Tell your attorney to proceed without delay. Once a mortgagor's attitude towards his responsibility has deteriorated to a point where you feel compelled to make foreclosure noises, you have passed the point of no return. If he does not shape up and fulfill the promises he made, and you back down without following through on the threats you have made, you will lose what little control you might still have retained.

No Is the Best Policy

No matter how awesome your correspondence, how ruthless your attorney, or how purple your ire when roused, the most effective technique for encouraging prompt payments is adamantly refusing to extend loans to poor risks.

If your applicant's credit report shows that three retailers, one physician, and two public utilities found it necessary to retain counsel in an effort to collect moneys due them from him within the past two years, be assured that no letter, however lyrical, and no conference, however inspiring, will make a silk purse out of your sow's ear.

Your greatest opportunity to achieve an impressive average of prompt payments is to eliminate the losers in advance.

Unfortunately, prospective dead-beats rarely carry identification. They wear no scarlet letters.

Most of them will be readily identified in the initial stages of analyzing the prospective loan. If this happens to you, consider yourself fortunate.

If their probable future delinquency becomes obvious during early interviews, and lack of firmness or an urge to play Santa Claus inhibits your ability to refuse the loan, color your future dismal.

Don't Expect Perfection

However firm you may be when circumstances warrant, your decision will be complicated by one confusing circumstance. An applicant's credit report will rarely mirror affluence. If his income were adequate to his needs, if his bills were all promptly paid as the due date approached, if his credit status brought a warm smile to retail credit managers, he generally would not be applying to you for a high interest loan secured by a mortgage on his family homestead.

Something is wrong, obviously. There's trouble in the air. Your task is not to find a trouble-free debtor, but rather one whose trouble is behind him.

Start your analysis with the knowledge that there must be a trouble spot somewhere. Your job is to find it.

Phil and Ralph

Phil's wife had a serious operation and an extended convalescence, using all his emergency funds and eating into current income. How is she now? Back on her feet. The husband? Still senior foremen at the plant. Been there twenty-one years come August.

Ralph had been laid off at the plant because the suppliers were on strike. Seventeen weeks without a pay check. He managed fine for the first three months, but then the savings gave out and he had to hold off paying some bills. The local newspapers announced yesterday that the plant would reopen Monday. A veteran skilled lathe operator, he will be among the first to report back.

Both applicants sound fine. Sure, each credit report has a few blotches, but the problems that arose were certainly not of their own making. They both have steady incomes and can be expected to straighten out with a boost from you.

Looks Like a Blue Chip

Raymond is a dynamic young executive, college trained, starting up the ladder of an eminent local corporation. He is doing well and creating a good impression. His entertainment pattern has resulted in a sizable overdue bill at one of the nicer suburban liquor shops. His eagerness to look the part of a promising family man destined for better things has resulted in overdue accounts at one haberdashery store and two specialty shops. He owns a late model luxury compact automobile, and his wife drives a shining new station wagon. They anticipate being able to afford the suburban home they live in as soon as the next raise comes through. And there seems to be little doubt that the raise will materialize. He's a dynamo. His wife is a charmer. Their children are beautifully clothed and well behaved. Their inquiry presents you with an opportunity to add some class to your portfolio.

Give someone else the privilege. Raymond and his family have just started a life-long career of living substantially above their income. Certainly that income will rise dramatically, but never quite as vigorously as their spending habits. He may make it some day, become a senior vice president, and have the income, at long last, to live as his ambition dictates. But his life will be a tight-rope walk for twenty years. One misstep and — splash! — egg all over his face. His pattern is based upon spending today what he hopes to achieve the day after tomorrow. If his precarious climb to success is somehow delayed by unanticipated adversity, his entire facade will collapse. The house of cards will topple. This man will continually create his own emergencies. Look elsewhere.

Becoming a Partner

George is an engineer, a competent man who has achieved a comfortable niche. His employer values him highly, his creditors wish they had a dozen more like him. He lives well and meets all his bills. Happy as he is at the plant, George has always yearned to go into business for himself. Now he has an idea. He's invented a product that he knows every golfer in America will buy. All he needs is five thousand dollars to form a corporation, make a half-dozen samples, and begin distribution. Just one-fifth of the income George confidently expects from his invention will more than cover his monthly payment. The Safety Formula works out to 91% + $1,100, but you're as excited about the invention as George is, and are willing to accept his corporate share in the invention as security. Let's face it, it isn't often that you have an opportunity to become associated with something as exciting as this.

If it's excitement you want, try a good movie.

What you are considering doing is financing a business, a particularly risky business. And make no mistake about it, you are not being invited to share the benefits if success rears its unlikely head. If George hits the bull's eye, he gets rich and you get the same interest rate all your clients have been paying for years. If George falls flat on his face, then you share in the benefits. He loses some pride, and you lose your five thousand dollars.

It will not be a total loss, of course. Your wife will undoubtedly have the corporate stock framed and hung in your den. Every time someone visits, she will lead the chorus of belly laughs. And you will probably receive a half dozen of "The Golfer's Friend." Very possibly the original half dozen no one would buy.

Lend money only when it is amply secured by real estate. Never accept pie-in-the-sky.

16

Other Means Of
Mortgage Investment

Purchase Money Mortgages ... Making an Offer ... Analyzing
the Benefits ... Comparing the Old with the New ... A Stranger's
Note ... A Clue to Tomorrow ... Buying a Portfolio ... An
Affidavit ... Exotic Variations ... The Balloon ... The Balloon
Bursts ... Play It Again, Sam

Purchase Money Mortgages

You may not be aware of it, but there are a great many private
mortgages in existence.

A private mortgage is one granted by an individual or group other
than a public bank or corporation.

A purchase money mortgage is a fine example of a private mortgage. It is offered by the owner of a piece of property to facilitate its
sale.

Many such purchase money mortgages exist. They are not at all
uncommon. They are, however, relatively unprofitable. In his eagerness to consummate the sale of his home, the property owner rarely
charges above the existing institutional mortgage interest rate, and
sometimes charges less, as an inducement to sign.

After the property has been sold, and the modest monthly checks
in payment of the purchase money mortgage begin to arrive, many
mortgagees become restless. Their money is tied up for three, five, ten,

or sometimes fifteen years. They start to think of the vacation they could have if they had their mortgage money in a single lump sum.

Some look for buyers. Others do not. But their restlessness, their lack of patience, makes them prime targets for an offer to purchase.

How would you go about buying an existing purchase money mortgage?

Making an Offer

Offer to pay cash, right now, in exchange for an assignment of the mortgage.

Such an assignment would entitle you to collect all the remaining payments due the original mortgagee on the existing mortgage.

The amount of cash to be offered is geared either to the customary second mortgage interest rate in your community, or the idiosyncrasies of your potential vendor.

Unless he is active in the local money market, your potential vendor will not be the least bit impressed by customary business patterns. In spite of the general wide acceptance of, say, a 20 per cent discount, he may become infuriated when you offer $1,600 for his $2,000 mortgage.

On the other hand, he may consider $1,500 a fair offer.

You will never know if you do all the talking. Keep quiet and listen after introducing the subject.

Tell him that you are interested in paying cash for the mortgage he holds on his former home. Don't forget to add that when you buy the mortgage, you will be assuming the inconvenience and risk of collecting the payments as they become due. Because of the possible difficulties involved, you cannot pay him the entire balance due. You would expect him to offer you a discount.

Now, just keep quiet and listen. Some mortgage holders love that little ol' mortgage and couldn't bear to part with it. Some would not mind assigning it to you, but at a discount so small as to be microscopic.

Some mortgage holders have been waiting for a rich idiot like you to come along. They can smell that Florida vacation. Their minds rapidly calculate the cost of a trip South. The mortgage has a $1,905 balance. They figure $1,600 would be ample for their vacation needs, and try it on for size.

"Sixteen hundred dollars?"

Analyzing the Benefits

Well, let's work it out. Originally the mortgage may have been for $3,000 at 6 per cent for five years. Three years, or thirty-six payments, remain, and the current balance is $1,905.00.

The payments are $58.00 a month.

$$
\begin{array}{r}
\$58.00 \\
\underline{\text{x36 payments}} \\
34800 \\
\underline{17400} \\
\$2,088.00 \text{ moneys due} \\
\underline{-1,600.00 \text{ cost}} \\
\$488.00 \text{ profit}
\end{array}
$$

If the normal rate of return in your community is 10 per cent, trot out your loan amortization booklet.

10%	1 year	2 years	3 years
$1,200	$105.50	$55.38	$38.73
1,300	114.30	59.99	41.95
1,400	123.09	64.61	45.18
1,500	131.88	69.22	48.41
1,600	140.67	73.84	51.63
1,700	149.46	78.45	54.86
1,800	158.25	83.07	58.09

A $1,600 loan, the cash you are investing, for three years at 10 per cent would carry thirty-six payments at $51.63.

$$
\begin{array}{r}
\$51.63 \\
\underline{\text{x }36 \text{ payments}} \\
309\ 78 \\
\underline{1,548\ 9} \\
\$1,858.68
\end{array}
$$

The advantage is considerable. Thirty-six payments at $58.00 a month produce a total of $2,088 if paid to conclusion. Thirty-six payments at $51.63 (six dollars and thirty-seven cents more per month) produce a total of $1,858.68 if paid to conclusion.

$2,088.00 discounted purchase money mortgage
−1,858.68 10% mortgage
$ 229.32

You win by two hundred twenty-nine dollars and thirty-two cents. Not bad.

What if the mortgage holder offered it to you for $1,700? Should you accept his offer in a community where a 10 per cent return is common?

Figure it out, using the same 10 per cent chart referred to earlier.

Comparing the Old with the New

That certainly sounds simple. Much less mumbo-jumbo than the intricacies of creating a new mortgage.

Nonsense.

There is absolutely no difference between purchasing a mortgage and creating one, at least as far as employing safeguards are concerned.

You must still examine the mortgagor's credit report to assure yourself that he is a decent risk.

You must still obtain an appraisal of the property to enable you to apply the Safety Formula.

You must still apply the Ability-to-Pay Formula, check his insurance policy, order a Change Endorsement, and follow all the other steps I outlined earlier.

There are some differences, however. Some good, some bad.

A Stranger's Note

The mortgage note will not be your own. It may not guarantee you a minimum period of interest payments. Well, the absence of such a limitation is to your benefit, in this case.

The sooner your transferred mortgagor pays the full balance of the mortgage, the sooner you earn the $305 bonus you achieved by buying the $1,905 mortgage for $1,600. If he takes a full thirty-six months, you earn a bonus of $8.47 a month, plus interest. If he pays it off in four months, your bonus earnings shoot up to $76.25 a month, plus interest.

Encourage your new debtor to pay the full balance of his loan as soon as possible. You might even offer him an inducement, a fifty dollar rebate for early prepayment, or a hundred dollar reduction.

The mortgage note might not call the entire balance due in the event the mortgagor transfers the property.

In that case, having carefully examined and evaluated your new mortgagor, you might suddenly find that he has been replaced by a poor credit risk, an alcoholic, or a man whose hobby seems to be drawing checks on insufficient funds. Unless your note protects you, there is very little you can do.

The mortgage note might not include costs of collection and reasonable attorney's fees.

The mortgage note might not insist that the mortgagor keep the premises insured for your benefit and to your satisfaction.

There are many similar and valuable rights included in the sample note in Chapter 13 that may be excluded from the note you are considering purchasing.

Keep those omissions in mind. Recognize the increased risks they create. Evaluate the attractiveness of your investment return in terms of the protection you must forfeit.

Keep in mind, too, that you must have your own attorney run down the title to the mortgage to be certain that your seller has the right to transfer it.

A Clue to Tomorrow

There is one marked superiority of the purchase of an existing second mortgage, however. An existing mortgage has a history.

The mortgage may be almost two years old. That means approximately twenty-four payments should have been received.

Ask to see your seller's records. Check the dates of receipt. Were they mailed promptly? Did any checks bounce?

I have never known a mortgage investor who did not keep records of the payments he received. If your prospect claims to have none, don't believe him. Assume the record is a bad one and he has chosen not to share it with you. Beware!

Buying a Portfolio

Occasionally you will find mortgage investors seeking to sell their mortgage portfolio.

Examine the payment records. If they look good, question the investor about the size of the first mortgage. Ask if he has seen the house, and if he has an appraisal. He may have ordered a credit report. Ask to see it.

Treat the portfolio exactly as you would any new mortgage. Be conservative.

You should not expect any sizable discount from an investor, particularly if the interest rate reflects the normal second mortgage rate of your community.

I suggest that you try to get a modest discount, though, the equivalent of your community's mortgage brokers' commission. By purchasing his portfolio, or a portion of it, you are functioning as a broker would.

If the mortgage balance if $1,500 and the standard broker's commission is 2 per cent, try to pay $1,470

If it is necessary for you to incur expenses beyond the thirty dollar discount, you should demand a discount at least equal to your out-of-pocket costs. Otherwise, if your jurisdiction permits the mortgagor to pay some of those costs, you will be paying a premium. Keep in mind that you will certainly have some costs: Credit report, appraisal, recording of the assignment of mortgage, etc.

An Affidavit

There is one form of protection that applies only to the purchase of a preexisting second mortgage.

It is virtually impossible to determine the actual balance of an existing mortgage. Occasionally, mortgagors pay in advance. I know of one mortgagor, strangely enough, who consistently paid one year in advance.

In any event, it is important that you be assured the mortgage balance quoted is accurate.

Have the seller sign an affidavit.

AFFIDAVIT

This is to certify that the mortgage dated June 16, 19--, from John W. Doe to Richard Y. Roe, and recorded in the Land Records of the Town of XYZ at Volume 47, page 293, in the original amount of $3,000, has a balance due of $1,905 as of August 1, 19--, with interest thereon at 6 per cent per annum from said first day of August.

Attached hereto are the original note and deed of said mortgage.

I make this affidavit knowing that Frank Z. Foe will rely upon the information herein in the purchase of said mortgage.

_____   _____

date   Richard Y. Roe

Exotic Variations

There is an endless variety of enticing deviations from the equal monthly payment method of amortizing a loan.

I discussed the variations briefly in an earlier chapter, taking the time at that early stage primarily to scare you away.

Now that you have followed me through more that fifteen chapters of mortgage theory and mortgage practice, you are entitled to a detailed discussion of one of the more sophisticated aspects of mortgage investment.

Please understand. I have not changed my mind. I still do not feel that you should undertake any trips in radically designed crafts. It is to your benefit to keep your payment patterns simple, except in extraordinary circumstances.

Some variations might be of interest, however.

A solvent home-owner, proud possessor of a rather small mortgage, is eager to invest $2,000 in a business side-line. Realistic about his prospects, he admits that he cannot expect any return for at least nine months, perhaps ten.

His house is easily worth $25,000. He has shown you his latest mortgage bill. Balance: $11,672.49. Add a $2,000 second mortgage and your Safety Formula reads 54.7 per cent with a margin of $11,328.

He is a junior executive at the local plant, starting up the ladder to Big Wheel. His salary amply covers the demands of our Ability-to-Pay Formula.

The proposal: "Give me $2,000 now. I'll sign the note and the mortgage. You record them. I'll pay only interest for twelve months and then retire the loan in forty-eight consecutive equal monthly payments of principal and interest."

What say you, O Magnificent Mortgagee?

Well, obviously, this applicant is a blue chip. His 54 per cent Safety Formula is a delight. His income would enable him to repay your loan without the benefit of any return on his investment. His position in the community compels him to maintain a good record.

The payment of only interest for twelve months means maximum earnings for you during the first year.

Sounds good to me.

The same general outline, containing just a few less attractive statistics, could be a very dangerous investment, however. Proceed with caution. And never hesitate to wait for the next opportunity.

The Balloon

One major form of second mortgage is the balloon mortgage, its colorful name graphically reflecting the small initial payments and the large final payment: the big, fat balloon.

Ed Eager wants to borrow $4,000. He cannot afford the normal five-year monthly payment, but he is certain he could afford to make monthly payments for fifty-nine months at the rate of a ten-year mortgage, and then pay the entire balance due in the final month of the fifth year, the sixtieth payment.

After fifty-nine payments at a ten-year amortization rate, Ed might owe $2,600.

That's the problem. Ed Eager couldn't afford to pay a slightly larger monthly payment. How in the world is he going to come up with twenty-six hundred dollars?

There is one common, and relatively legitimate answer. Balloon mortgages are most often employed as purchase money mortgages in the transfer of investment real estate: apartment houses, office buildings, shopping centers.

In such circumstances, the balloon is commonly postponed to the seventh, eighth, or tenth years. The monthly payments prior to the large balloon payment are often based on a fifteen, twenty, or even twenty-five year mortgage term.

Such an arrangement accomplishes a varied number of purposes:

(a) The smaller monthly payment on the second mortgage enables the buyer to show a maximum return on his cash investment.

(b) By encouraging the use of artificially lowered monthly second mortgage payments, the seller is able to command a higher price for his investment property.

(c) At the conclusion of the seventh, eighth, or tenth year, the buyer has reduced the balance of both his first and second mortgage to a level lower than the original amount of his first mortgage. The buyer remortgages his property at least back to the original level of his first mortgage, pays the balloon, and pockets the difference.

The Balloon Bursts

Sounds idyllic.

Unfortunately, in times of rising interest rates it can be catastrophic. Picture a buyer enjoying a twenty-five year first mortgage at five and a half per cent who eight years later finds that he can do no better than a twenty-year mortgage at six and a quarter per cent - and must pay a fee of two per cent of the mortgage principal for the privilege. Idyllic?

But back to Ed Eager. He's not a real estate investor. Ed is an average sort of a guy who had a great idea to rake in a bundle of money. A pizza stand. How could he miss? Four thousand dollars was all he needed for the down payment on fixtures, security deposit for the rent, ovens and supplies. In eight years, when the balloon became due, Ed would just dip into his bundle and pay up.

But the shop folded. Ed lost all his equipment after making payments for four years. and still owes about $1,500 for supplies.

What can you do? Foreclose? In spite of all the hardships Ed suffered, he never missed one monthly payment.

Play It Again, Sam

There is a solution, of course. It's the standard approach at balloon time. Write a new mortgage for the balance of the money due.

It's a mortgage you certainly are not eager to have. Unfortunately, unless you can find someone else willing to lend Ed the money, you will have no choice but to accept a man whose current economic status makes him a perfectly horrendous risk. If you had not backed yourself into a corner by agreeing to write a balloon mortgage, you would not be feeling sorry for yourself now.

The problem may be even more terrifying. Ed's creditors may have attached his house. If there are liens on his property subsequent to your mortgage, you cannot rewrite it. To do so would entail releasing the mortgage, which would move the liens up one position, and then recording a new mortgage behind the liens.

You may have to consider increasing the new mortgage to an amount high enough to settle the accounts of the attaching creditors. Then they would release their liens and your new mortgage would hold its place in line.

Balloons are fine at parades and birthday parties. They have no place in a mature adult's mortgage portfolio.

17

Building Your Portfolio

The Pace Accelerates ... Invitations to Renew ... Dealing with a
Name Brand ... A Shifting Safety Formula ... Bread Cast upon
the Waters ... Relax ... Money Is Always in Style ... Like
Rabbits ... Checking vs. Savings Accounts ... Shifting into Higher Gear

The Pace Accelerates

After you have invested in a number of mortgages and have begun
to gather a series of monthly payments, it becomes necessary to
accelerate your investment pattern.

Your money is accumulating at a rapid pace and, although you are
being careful to deposit the mortgage checks and your weekly savings
in a manner that will provide a maximum return, much of your success
will be determined by the speed with which you are able to reinvest
your funds.

I assume you are using the techniques discussed in Chapter 5 to
locate mortgage opportunities.

There is one approach we have not yet discussed, a technique
available only to those who already have mortgages in force.

Invitations to Renew

If your mortgage guarantees you twelve months of interest, check
those mortgages that have been outstanding more than one year. If

your guarantee is for twenty-four months, check those mortgages that have already celebrated their second anniversary.

Have any of them been particularly prompt? Whether their promptness results from your proding or by reason of their own fine sense of responsibility is irrelevant.

If their payment pattern is good, I suggest that you make them aware their promptness is noted and appreciated, and at the same time take a major step towards building your portfolio — all for the same postage stamp.

A letter along the following lines will accomplish both objectives:

Dear Mr. and Mrs. Mortgagor:

As I mentioned when the mortgage was placed upon your home, prompt monthly payments are of importance to me.

Your payment pattern has been excellent. It is a pleasure dealing with you.

As a result of your promptness, I stand ready to increase your mortgage to its original amount, or a bit higher, whenever you ask.

Very truly,

Letters of this sort are an incentive to continue timely payments. Knowing their efforts are appreciated is a spur to the mortgagor. In addition, experience indicates that almost 50 per cent of the accounts approached in this manner act upon the offer sooner or later.

Some will react immediately. Others may wait six months or a year. The overall reaction is generally great enough to warrant the preparation and mailing of these "thank you" letters on a regular basis.

Dealing with a Name Brand

Do not overlook the fact that an existing mortgagor whose payment record is fine enough to warrant an invitation to renew or expand his mortgage is superior to the applicant who answers your advertisement, or is recommended by a friend. You know how seriously the existing mortgagor views his obligation. You can only guess how responsible the new applicant may prove to be.

Add to this the fact that by renewing the mortgage back to the original amount, your Safety Formula must inevitably show a percentage superior to the results obtained when you first granted him a mortgage. While he has been decreasing the balance of your mortgage, he has also been pecking away at the balance of his original mortgage.

As a matter of fact, you can increase the second mortgage to an amount equal to the original second mortgage balance, together with diminution of the first mortgage principal balance since originating the second mortgage. The Safety Formula will not change.

A Shifting Safety Formula

Originally:

First mortgage balance	$17,895
Second mortgage	2,000
	$19,895

Appraised value $31,500

$$\begin{array}{r} .63 = 63\% \\ 315\,\overline{\smash{)}198.95} \\ \underline{189\ 0} \\ 9\ 95 \\ \underline{9\ 45} \\ 50 \end{array}$$

$31,500
−19,895
$11,605

Safety Formula: 63% + $11,605

Some Time later:

First mortgage balance: $17,136
Second mortgage balance: 1,257

To return second mortgage to original $2,000 balance, add $743.

To return first mortgage to balance when second mortgage originated, add $759.

Thus, you may add $1,502 to the $1,257 current second mortgage balance without any variation in the original Safety Formula.

$1,257 Current second mortgage balance
   743 Diminution in second mortgage balance
   759 Diminution in first mortgage balance
$2,759 New second mortgage balance
17,136 Current first mortgage balance
$19,895
Using same appraised value: $31,500

$$
\begin{array}{r}
.63\% \ + \ \$11,605 \\
315\overline{)\ 198.95} \\
189\ 0 \\
\overline{9\ 95} \\
9\ 45 \\
\overline{50}
\end{array}
$$

$$
\begin{array}{r}
\$31,500 \\
-\ 19,895 \\
\hline
\$11,605
\end{array}
$$

Results: Your mortgagor is pleased. He has been permitted to raise a considerable amount of additional cash in a short period of time.

You are gratified. You have kept your mortgage funds working and have invested them with someone who has proved that he honors his obligations.

One point. Check your Ability-to-Pay Formula. Although the first mortgage payment remains the same, the larger second mortgage will result in a higher monthly payment, unless the term is increased accordingly.

Bread Cast upon the Waters

One prime source of new borrowers may well be your competitors in the community, if such exist. You will discover who they are as you become more involved in your investments.

Assume for a moment that a prospect has approached you for a loan at a time when you are completely bereft of funds.

There is nothing to be gained by merely advising him that you cannot be of service at this time. Take his telephone number and tell him that you will return his call in a few moments.

Call a competitor who might have been helpful, or who has a potential for cooperation. Explain that you have a prospect you must refuse because all your funds are invested at the moment. It seems a shame not to make full use of the opportunity. You thought he might welcome a referral.

Such an overture can result in a mutually beneficial reciprocal relationship in the months and years to come, either in applicants or advice.

Call the applicant, explain the situation, and he, too, will welcome the referral.

Everybody's happy.

Relax

There is one major problem that must be carefully understood. This chapter, discussing building your portfolio, is an appropriate launching pad.

Our economy runs in cycles. The stock market runs in cycles. Second mortgages run in cycles, too.

You must, at all costs, refuse to panic during slow periods. You may be in the market for a new mortgage for nine weeks before an appropriate applicant appears. Not just three, or six, but nine long weeks. During that time applicants will still come to your attention.

The temptation to get another mortgage on the books, to get your excess funds to work as soon as possible, may push you into poor judgment.

Stand fast. When the qualified applicants do begin to call, there will be as many as you can handle. If you use your money to sign a poor prospect, you will have none available when a blue chip calls.

Money Is Always in Style

The drought may continue for months. Fortunately, the Internal Revenue Service asks those who are self-employed to make quarterly tax payments. That helps. Detroit can always be counted on to produce new models every year. Another aid. The summer months mean vacations. Spring and fall mean college tuition. Winter means Christmas. Don't become discouraged. In this affluent society of ours, there are tens of thousands of specialists perfecting techniques to put us in debt. It's the American way. And an unbelievable number of us play our roles to the hilt. With gusto.

Be patient.

Like Rabbits

Money, like rabbits, has the facility of rapidly reproducing itself. Nine per cent interest reinvested at   9   per cent interest, banked between use, and used as a basis for a line of credit, soon turns a modest trickle into a bubbling brook.

This reproductive capacity of capital is activated only by astute management techniques. The next chapter details the acceleration powers of the use of credit.

As a necessary preliminary to building your portfolio, you must understand why and how the portfolio growth develops.

Monthly mortgage payments and weekly savings, properly managed, will earn a modest return if you forego the convenience of maintaining a checking account as the depository. It is obviously very handy to be able to draw checks from your special account to meet investment expenses or transfer funds to a new mortgagor. But the convenience is not without its cost.

Your account will be charged for each transaction, whether deposit or withdrawal. The charges will be modest, of course, but however modest they may be, they represent a diminution of your available investment funds.

Savings accounts are based upon a completely different philosophy. There is no charge for deposits. There is no monthly charge for maintaining the account. Most savings accounts permit one check a month to be drawn against the balance without charge. Savings accounts, of course, pay you for the privilege of having your funds at hand.

Checking vs. Savings Accounts

Thus, maintaining your money in a checking account becomes more costly as it is compared with its alternative, banking the funds in an interest-bearing savings account.

The cost of a small checking account may be only ten dollars a year, but the net earnings available as a result of banking those modest funds may be twenty-five dollars a year. The net loss to you is now thirty-five dollars, rather than ten.

Unless you are an active investor, you may find that one check a month will meet your needs. Draw it from your savings account the day of your mortgage closing to cover the mortgage itself and all of the expenses for which you are responsible: the credit report, the loan reduction schedule, the mortgage broker's commission, or the appraiser's fee.

Your attorney will do the honors, breaking down your large check into the exact number necessary to complete the transactions and pay all the costs.

If you find that the system works well for you but that you seem to need two checks a month, split your savings and open another account.

Of course, when the occasion arises, you can compromise between the two extremes, withdraw the necessary amount and deposit it to your personal checking account for disbursement.

We have now progressed from the cost of a checking account to the income of a savings account, producing a net gain of some consequence. The next step is to accelerate that gain still further.

Shifting into a Higher Gear

The speed with which you transform relatively passive savings account funds into virile, dynamic mortgage investments will determine some of the speed with which your net worth will grow. Four or five per cent may be good. Eight or ten or twelve per cent is considerably better.

The problem is one of timing. You generally can anticipate when your savings will reach the level at which a new investment is possible. Don't wait until all the necessary funds are accumulated. A month or two before that happy day, begin to make the rounds. Set your machine in motion. Call your contacts. Or begin to run your newspaper advertisement again. In that way you will minimize the time lapse and maximize the earnings potential.

As your portfolio progresses, money will accumulate at an increasingly rapid rate. There will soon be shorter periods of time between investment levels. You may find that you cannot afford to allow your machinery to idle. What with existing mortgagors periodically prepaying their debts, a larger flow of monthly payments, applicants who contact you on their own initiative, and mortgagors seeking to renew their loans, you may find that competent management compels a continuous program of actively seeking new investments.

Your purpose is to keep at an absolute minimum the time during which your funds are earning the modest interest rates of local savings banks or loan associations.

18

Accelerating Your Growth

Leverage vs. Your Own Funds ... A Closer Look ... Expanding
Your Inventory ... Tread Cautiously ... Cash on the Line ...
Banker's Revenge ... Start Modestly and Start Now ... Now
Play for Real ... Earn Now, Pay Later ... The Borrower's Bonus
... The Velvet Trap ... The Mechanics of Compounding ... The
Limits of Leverage ... Caution ... Investment Group Advantages
... Investment Group Danger ... Recommended Form of Loan
Agreement

Leverage vs. Your Own Funds

Compare two investors: L. E. Verage and Owen Funds. Mr. Owen
Funds is a prudent man. He carefully sets aside ten dollars each week
to add to his modest nest egg of three thousand dollars in surplus
savings. The surplus and weekly savings are carefully invested in
mortgages that score well in Safety Formula and Ability-to-Pay tests.
Mr. Owen Funds extends his mortgage investment portfolio as far as
his funds permit, but cautiously never expands his investments beyond
those funds. His net worth grows steadily.

Mr. L. E. Verage is also a prudent man, blessed with the same
savings surplus, the ability to supplement his savings by ten dollars
each week, and a sound knowledge of conservative mortgage investment techniques. He does employ one approach that shocks Owen
Funds, however, an approach that accelerates his growth to a degree
beyond that enjoyed by Owen Funds.

L. E. Verage uses other people's money to supplement his own.

Why? Because a mortgage investor with four thousand dollars in mortgage loans outstanding will have a far greater potential for profit than the investor having three thousand dollars in mortgages, particularly if each of the investors has only three thousand dollars of his own money involved.

A Closer Look

Let's look at it this way: Three thousand dollars invested at 10 per cent for three years will produce $96.81 a month, or a gross profit of $485.16 in thirty-six months. At the same time, of course, ten dollars in savings will be added to the kitty each week.

Four thousand dollars invested under the same circumstances will produce thirty-six payments of $129.07 a month. In six months, the repayments will total $774.42. Add the weekly ten dollars savings and, in those same six months you will collect another $260 for a total of $1,034.42.

If your thousand dollars was borrowed from a commercial bank at 6 per cent per annum, to be paid back at the end of six months, your total repayment would be the original $1,000 and one-half of the 6 per cent annual interest rate, or 3 per cent. Repayment is thus $1,030. Money on hand, $1,034.42.

In this simple, very simple, example, who has the financial advantage, Owen Funds or L. E. Verage?

At the conclusion of the first six months, Owen Funds has received $580.86 in monthly payments, plus $260 in his own weekly savings, or $840.86 cash on hand and $2,904.30 due from the remaining thirty monthly payments, a total of $3,745.16.

L. E. Verage will have only $4.42 cash on hand, having used his first six month's weekly savings, but he will have $3,872.10 due from the remaining monthly payments, for a total of $3,876.52.

His six-month loan resulted in an additional $131.36 in interest.

Expanding Your Inventory

L. E. Verage was applying the very same principle to money that retail merchants apply to inventory. The butcher might buy meat for

$1.00 a pound and sell it for $1.50. The supermarket might buy soda for $2.40 a case of twenty-four and sell the bottles for 15 cents apiece.

L. E. Verage bought money for 6 per cent and sold it at 10 . He went one step further. He used the income from his increased inventory of money to liquidate the loan. Thus, he did much more than merely buy at 6 per cent what he sold at 10 . He paid 6 per cent for only six months and earned 10 per cent for three years. Obviously, he enjoyed a great advantage.

Of course, he has still another advantage. By borrowing a modest sum and repaying promptly, L. E. Verage established a fine history with the bank's loan officer. If he chose to repeat that transaction a short while later, the bank would accommodate him. Within the period of three years used in our example, L. E. Verage could repeat the pattern three or four times. He might even increase the amount of the loan, as his pattern of prompt repaying was established, and as his net worth grew.

With each subsequent loan, providing he is wise enough to borrow only when a qualified mortgagor is waiting in the wings, L. E. Verage would increase the amount of monthly payments flowing towards him. Rather than be limited to having his own $3,000 in mortgage loans generating monthly payments, subsequent loans would increase his portfolio, creating even more in monthly mortgage payments. An increased flow means either he would be capable of borrowing the next thousand dollars for a shorter period of time, decreasing the interest cost, or he would be able to increase the amount of the loan to be repaid in those six months.

In either event, L. E. Verage wins. His margin of profit increases.

Tread Cautiously

Before you react to this rather primitive example of the benefits of leverage, or the use of other people's funds, please take note of this caveat.

Going into debt to finance mortgage investments, or any other form of investment, can be suicidal. Idiots do it regularly. Many bankrupt businessmen were skilled practitioners of the art. A high percentage of the bodies hurtling to the pavement from the upper windows of Wall Street in 1929 had practiced leverage. Buying on margin is the stock market's euphemism for using other people's money.

If ever a mortgage investor were to follow my recommendations for exercising prudence in investment judgment, the leveraging mortgagee must head the list. By using borrowed funds you certainly do increase your opportunity to gain. But just as surely, you increase your potential loss.

If the second mortgages in which Owen Funds invested his three thousand dollars were to turn sour and prove valueless, his loss would be three thousand dollars.

Had L. E. Verage borrowed his additional thousand dollars to increase his margin of profit, however, and chosen poor investment vehicles, he would lose his three thousand dollars, owe the bank an additional thousand dollars, and owe that same bank the interest due on the thousand dollar loan. His potential loss soars above $4,000.

Scared?

Good! If you're not scared, you're not very bright.

The moral of this macabre tale is that the conservative approach to mortgage investment stressed throughout this book is a necessary basis, an absolute requirement, for anyone seeking to expand his profits by using borrowed funds.

If you are wise enough not to be too smart, if you are cautious enough not to be too flippant, leverage is a technique that can prove to be extraordinarily rewarding.

Just keep in mind that I did not elect to discuss this topic towards the end of the book by chance. It was the result of considered judgment. Investing borrowed funds should never precede complete, total mastery of the investment program.

Cash on the Line

There are two great masses of people in our nation, those who use credit as a normal financing technique and those quaint souls who buy only when they have the cash available.

The cash buyers are an exotic race, fast disappearing from the face of the earth. Their demise seems to sadden no one, other than the stern moralists or the abstract economic philosophers. The diminishing whooping cranes cause more anguish than the disappearing cash-on-the-liners.

If you have already used credit, if your automobile was financed by a bank loan, or your furniture was bought on time, your rating has been established. You are a known quantity. If you paid promptly, if your checks were in the proper amounts, your credit history will recommend you to the loan officer.

On the other hand, if you waited until the collection letters arrived, or an attorney called before you honored your obligation, your reception will be a cool one. You had better begin again, if you can, in a small way, and establish a new rating. It will require patience and promptness. With the passage of time, however, and exemplary attention to your payment schedules, you will resurrect your status.

Banker's Revenge

For those of you who have always proudly met your needs with payment in full on the barrelhead, the road will be equally long and hard. You are an odd-ball. Worse, you have no references.

If you had paid for your storm windows in twenty-four easy, but swollen, monthly payments, the loan officer would have some insight into your fiscal responsibility. If you had foregone the savings when you bought the new bedroom set and signed a note, your cavalier attitude would have been rewarded by a credit rating.

Instead, you chose to deny the credit industry their pound of flesh. Now, Buster, they extract their revenge.

Nothing is quite as pitiful as a loan officer interviewing an applicant who had always imagined cash payments to be a sign of financial superiority. Well, if not superiority, then certainly stability.

Times have changed. Financial stability today is installing a swimming pool before you have the money and somehow managing to successfully meet each installment.

Start Modestly and Start Now

What should you do?

I suggest approaching the bank for a modest loan. Perhaps one thousand dollars. Do it before you have any need for the money. Do it now so that your credit will be established when the day arrives that you have need for the funds.

Borrowing money merely to establish a credit rating may be necessary, but it is frowned upon. It is preferred that you borrow funds to meet emergencies that arose as the result of poor money management. So, borrow the money to pay some doctor bills, an income tax statement, or your household bills.

Make certain that your loan does not call for monthly payments. Those are expensive. A 6 per cent personal loan calling for equal monthly payments costs approximately 12 per cent per annum. You can't make money that way.

You are looking for a single payment loan carrying a true annual interest rate.

Take the money and deposit it in a savings account in the bank or loan association paying the best interest rate in your community. Do your best to find one that pays interest from the date of your deposit to the date of your withdrawal. Otherwise, withdrawing your thousand dollars prior to the dividend date means the loss of all interest for the days during which it has been on deposit.

Let's assume a 60-day note. The charge is 6, or perhaps 7, per cent per annum. Your savings account will pay a related amount, of either 4 or 5 per cent. Thus, in sixty days, one sixth of a year, at 6 per cent per annum, the cost to you will be one-sixth of 6 per cent, 1 per cent, or ten dollars. The interest earnings, at 4 per cent per annum, will total six dollars and sixty-six cents.

It has cost you three dollars and thirty-four cents to establish a credit relationship.

Periodically repeat the process, all the while increasing the amount of your loan, extending the term of the loan, and earning the lender's warm regard.

Now Play for Real

Then, while a mortgagor stands in the wings, play the game for real. Borrow. Invest. Repay. Pocket the profits.

As I explained in one of the early chapters, banks do this all the time. They buy their product (money) at wholesale prices (interest on savings accounts) and sell at a profit (mortgages, personal loans). As a matter of fact, when you borrow from the bank, you help them to realize that profit. You are as much of a customer as the man who pays the florist a profit when he buys a dozen roses. Keep that in mind. It may help you to have a realistic attitude towards the loan officer. If you borrow periodically and repay promptly, you are not a burden, or a misfit seeking succor, you are a valued customer. His entire financial operation was created to cater to people such as you.

Don't apologize.

Earn Now, Pay Later

The rationale followed by most credit purchasers is an intriguing one. Why, they ask themselves, should I save my money for three years and then buy a new car? I can buy the new car now, then save my money, all the while enjoying the use of the car. It's the "fly now, pay later" syndrome.

To a degree, using borrowed funds to obtain leverage in your investment program is analogous to buying a refrigerator today and saving the money to pay for it while it is in use rather than postponing your pleasure until the money has been accumulated.

Of course, we substitute the income of an investment for the pleasure of a new appliance.

By borrowing money today to expand your investment income, you are using your future earnings and weekly savings before they have accumulated.

During the period of accumulation, you earn the difference between the bank's interest rate for your loan and the interest rate you are able to charge your mortgagor. Whatever the difference might be, it is all profit to you.

Then, after gathering monthly payments and weekly savings, you repay the loan. At that point, your interest payments to the bank cease, and your monthly payments from the mortgagor continues. The profit margin takes a satisfying leap forward.

The Borrower's Bonus

Viewed in another way, by borrowing you have established a format that compels you to reinvest your mortgage income and maintain your weekly savings program.

The extent to which you faithfully follow the reinvestment and savings program will determine much of your ultimate success. If a pattern of borrowing money, investment of the borrowed funds, and compulsive and timely repayment of that loss will assure the reinvestment of your monthly receipts and the accumulation of weekly savings, that alone is a sufficient basis for expanding your investment portfolio by means of borrowed funds.

There are four keys to the acceleration of your investment program:

1. Make regular additions to your investment fund.
2. Keep your investment funds working at all times.
3. Reinvest your earnings.
4. Use other people's money.

If the fourth key, using other people's money, will be used in a way that assures use of the first and third keys, the profit motive becomes a bonus, and borrowed funds become a superb investment technique.

The Velvet Trap

Unfortunately, the skills of the advertising industry are so finely honed that our possessions never seem to keep up with our desires. We constantly seek more than we possess, and often more than our incomes warrant. Thus, dissipation of monthly mortgage investment checks are a great temptation, as are foregoing the weekly packets of savings destined for your investment fund. I cannot dispute the fact that those moneys would look much nicer in a new sports car or summer home. The point is, that although a steadily increasing mortgage portfolio may never win a blue ribbon at the Modern Museum, it will bring comfort and security to your entire family when college tuition, a medical emergency, or a long awaited retirement come to pass.

If you siphon off any of the mortgage income, you defeat the dynamics of compounded interest. A 9 per cent mortgage may produce an attractive return, but when you invest those 9 per cent earnings at 9 per cent, then the results begin to glow.

If the earnings are not reinvested, it will take a bit more than eleven years at 9 per cent for you to earn an amount equal to your original investment. If you retain the earnings and reinvest them annually, you will double your money in eight years, almost 30 per cent sooner.

The Mechanics of Compounding

To aid you in appreciating the power of compound interest, here is a chart showing how long it takes to double your money at different rates of interest. Because this chart is based upon only an annual compounding of interest, you will produce superior results by arranging your investment program so that you compound your earnings more often.

Interest Return	Approximate Period of Years
6%	12
7%	10¼
8%	9
9%	8
10%	7¼
11%	6⅔
12%	6⅛

In order to compute the number of years it will take to double your money at any rate of interest, compounded annually, divide 69.3 by the interest rate and add 0.35.

To find out the interest rate necessary to double your money in a particular span of years, reverse the process. Divide 69.3 by the number of years you have in mind, less 0.35.

The Limits of Leverage

One logical extension of the material covered in this chapter is a consideration of how much money you should borrow if you elect to apply the benefits of leverage to your mortgage portfolio.

We have discussed the absolute necessity of mastering prudent management techniques before borrowing investment funds, and we have also made it abundantly clear that leverage can be a two-edged sword.

Now, on to the arena.

I would suggest that you impose a limit of 50 per cent of the value of your portfolio. Because your mortgages represent very conservative investments, you will be securing your own indebtedness by an assets to liability ratio of two to one. The ratio will be endorsed by your banker when you have grown to the point of negotiating sizable loans and it amply protects you in the event of a temporary financial problem.

I recommend a second limitation. Borrow no more than the cash flow of mortgage income and your savings program will permit you to repay. Never extend your obligations beyond a readily demonstrable investment program income.

It is better to borrow less than you want than more than you can comfortably repay. Note, I said comfortably. The basic difference between you and your mortgagors is prudence. Keep it that way. Constantly applying an Ability-to-Pay Formula to your own leverage borrowing will protect your future.

Caution

One word of caution is to keep your mortgages small when your portfolio is a limited one. Although the Safety Formula, Ability-to-Pay Analysis, credit report, appraisal, and other techniques will assure you of solid investments, nothing is impossible. Be prepared. If lightning strikes and the improbable occurs when your entire protfolio consists of one twelve thousand dollar mortgage, your situation will be a serious one. Should a mortgage cause trouble when you have invested that same amount of money in eight fifteen-hundred dollar mortgages, you will weather the storm, particularly if the eight small mortgages are diversified as to geography, terms, and background of mortgagors.

Investment Groups Advantages

Investment groups have many advantages when they seek to borrow funds. The banker will be impressed to find a number of his regular accounts within the membership roster. Some may be stockholders as well as customers. A few will inevitably be prime accounts, the type he is eager to please.

Then, too, the cumulative net worth of the individuals comprising the group will often be impressive. When you set your individual assets to paper, you may find a moderate net worth of thirty thousand dollars. An investment group of fifteen men may average no more than you, but their total will be a very impressive $450,000.

Finally, a group of fifteen businessmen present an opportunity to a wide-awake bank officer. Prospects. New checking accounts. New savings accounts. New borrowers.

Investment Group Danger

There is one serious limitation to group loans, however. Your bank may attempt to use a form of loan agreement that employs joint and several liability. That is, if your partnership defaults, the bank may hold any single partner, or small group of partners, responsible for the entire debt. Naturally, the more affluent among the membership will resist the exposure.

Such an approach is unnecessary and unreasonable.

If you respect a 50 per cent of portfolio value as your loan limit, the bank will enjoy a two to one ratio of assets to debt. An analysis of your monthly mortgage income will show a comfortable margin of income over debt service.

If your analysis of partnership cash flow from mortgage payments as well as membership investment does not show ample means of meeting your loan obligation, lower your loan request until the cash flow is in line.

The form of group loan I favor provides for monthly principal payments and quarterly interest payments, the interest being at a true annual rate and applied to the average amount of principal outstanding during that quarter. The liability of each member is expressly limited to his proportionate share of the loan balance and interest due.

Recommended Form of Loan Agreement

One typical agreement negotiated with a lending institution follows. I recomend it to you.

AGREEMENT

This Agreement, made at   , this   day of
            , 19   , by and between   , a

partnership organized and existing under the laws of the State of
                                 , and having an office and place of business
in the Town of   in said State, hereinafter
referred to as Partnership, and   Bank and
Trust Company, a banking corporation organized under the laws of
the State of   , and having an office and place
of business in the Town of   in said State,
hereinafter referred to as Bank.

WITNESSETH:

Whereas, the Partnership wishes to borrow $
from the Bank and to give evidence of said indebtedness and security therefor; and

Whereas, the Bank desires to lend moneys to the Partnership;

Now, Therefore, in consideration of the premises and of the mutual promises each to the other made, it is agreed as follows:

1. An Executive Committee consisting of Messrs.
                                 , and
, shall represent the Partnership, and any of the aforementioned partners jointly signing such documents, instruments, notes, and papers as shall be required by the Bank to evidence any borrowings from the Bank and agreements in connection therewith, shall bind the Partnership and all of the partners.

2. The signers of this Agreement in the name of the Partnership comprise all of the partners thereof.

3. Every promissory note, or other evidence of debt or other security given on account of the Partnership signed, endorsed, accepted or executed as provided in this Agreement shall equally bind and obligate each and every partner of the Partnership to his pro rata share of the performance thereof, and each partner does hereby agree to the same; and it is further agreed that all assets of the Partnership are hereby pledged to the Bank, and any indebtedness of the Partnership created hereunder shall be a first lien on all of the assets of the Partnership.

4. The Bank shall give notice and made demand upon the Partnership by communicating with   , and the same shall be considered notice and demand to and upon all the partners.

5. The accrued liability hereunder of any partner shall survive his death, withdrawal from the Partnership, or termination of the Partnership; and this Agreement shall be binding upon the parties hereto, their heirs, executors, administrators, personal representatives and successors, as the case may be.

6. The Partnership shall pay the interest accrued on the average outstanding daily principal indebtedness owing to the Bank at the

end of each calendar quarter. And further, the Partnership shall pay to the Bank on or before the   day of each month one-twelfth (1/12) of the sum of the principal of such indebtedness.

In Witness Whereof, the   Bank and Trust Company has caused this instrument to be executed by   , its President hereunto duly authorized, and its corporate seal to be affixed, and the parties have hereunto set their hands and seal the day and year first above written.

Signed, Sealed and Delivered
   in the presence of:

THE   BANK AND TRUST COMPANY

By_____
                          Its President

HARTFORD CAPITAL FUND
By _____   _____

_____   _____
_____   _____
_____   _____
_____   _____

19

Protecting Your Investments

Maintain Standards ... A Rewrite ... New Evaluations ... Visit
the Scene ... Follow the Land Records ... Keep in Touch ...
Your Psychological Needs ... Swingers Need Not Apply ... No,
Virginia, Money Is Not Everything

Maintain Standards

There is more involved in safeguarding your mortgage investments
than depositing the mortgage deed and note in a secure place, although I must admit that such a deposit is as good a place to start this
chapter as I can recommend.

You protect your investment by holding fast to your standards, by
working with professionals skilled in their crafts, by maintaining a
tight rein on your mortgagors, by keeping adequate records, and by
wholeheartedly adopting a conservative pattern.

These safeguards are rather obvious. They have been clearly and
repeatedly outlined in earlier chapters.

Let's assume some rather common fact situations, however. Applicant seeks fifteen hundred dollars, three hundred and fifty dollars for
exterior coat of paint, and the balance for a concrete patio. Assuming
that he meets all our criteria, this is a very attractive loan. The money
he seeks will be used to protect the value of his home and, incidentally,
fortify our security. Theoretically. Approving the loan and transferring the funds will not assure you that the money will be used as
proposed. He might change his mind.

In a situation such as this, you protect your investment by with-holding the funds and communicating with the painter and mason. Tell them you have the money and will release it as soon as the job has been completed. When the work is finished, get the mortgagor's authorization to disburse the funds.

A Rewrite

Applicant has held your five-year mortgage for twenty-seven months now. He has repaid a significant portion of the principal and wishes to rewrite the mortgage, requesting that the new principal be one thousand dollars more than the original mortgage.

Let's be specific. Assume an original $1,500 mortgage. After twenty-seven months the mortgage balance has been reduced to $933.48. Your mortgagor wishes to rewrite the mortgage and raise it to twenty-five hundred dollars.

Thus, he is seeking $1,566.52 in gross cash, or twenty-five hundred dollars less $933.48.

The money he seeks is enough for you to add a new mortgage to your portfolio. What should you do?

First, check his payment record. When you extended him the loan, you were dealing with an unknown quantity. Yes, his credit report looks good, his income was ample, and he gave the impression of being sincere and responsible, but you could not be certain that he would meet his obligations promptly.

If he met twenty-seven payment dates in a responsible manner, chalk up a great big credit. He is now a known quantity. If you withheld the $1,566.52 he seeks in order to expand your portfolio by writing a new mortgage for a new applicant, you are exchanging an unknown quantity for someone experience has taught you is respon-sible.

If his payments have been slovenly, stop right there. Extending him further credit will serve only to convince him that all your speeches about prompt and full payment are so much hot air. His payment pattern, poor as it might have been before, will deteriorate still further if you reward his poor behavior with more money.

A mortgage renewal request gives you an opportunity to evaluate an applicant on the basis of experience rather than conjecture. Ex-ercise that opportunity.

New Evaluations

An existing mortgagor who seeks to rewrite his mortgage may have changed his job since your first credit report.

His new position might carry a lower salary scale, one so low that he no longer qualifies under the Ability-to-Pay Formula.

Protect your investment by ordering an up-to-date report.

The new mortgage for a larger sum will often involve a considerably higher monthly payment. If so, the Ability-to-Pay Formula must be recomputed. Don't ever become confused. Permitting someone to borrow more money than his income warrants is not a generous gesture. It is an invitation to disaster. The same man who promptly paid his monthly $43.07 second mortgage payment may be incapable of meeting a monthly $64.61 charge if his income is inadequate to the new pressure.

Incidentally, a larger sum may not involve a considerably higher monthly payment. If the original loan was for two years, and the new term is to be five years, the monthly payments may actually decrease.

If your mortgages are normally purchased through a broker, a renewal request is an opportunity to invest money without the expense of a broker's commission.

What about the Safety Formula? The figures have to change if your second mortgage investment increases. Let's assume a $19,000 appraisal, an $11,000 first mortgage, and your original supplemental mortgage of $1,500. The original Safety Formula would have read 66 per cent + $6,500. Now that you are contemplating adding an additional thousand dollars to the second mortgage, recompute your Safety Formula.

Visit the Scene

Your next step is to view the premises. Twenty-seven months is long enough for deterioration in the property itself or the retrogression of the surrounding community. Of course, you need not assume that an inspection will result in bad news. Your mortgagors may have added a garage in the interim, or completed their landscaping. The surrounding lots, formerly vacant, may now contain handsome homes.

Good news is a bonus, but satisfying as the additional security may be, bad news is your target. Added security, except under unusual circumstances, will not make a poor paying mortgagor a good risk. Diminished security could make an otherwise fine borrower a poor choice.

Bad news would be the key. Deterioration will undermine your Safety Formula. If, in the interim, a hamburger drive-in had been established on your mortgagor's northerly bound and a service station across the street, his $19,000 home might lose thirty-five hundred dollars of its prior value. With a $9,700 first mortgage, a $2,500 second mortgage, and a new $15,500 value, the Safety Formula dips to 81 per cent + $3,300. That's a long way from 64 per cent + $6,800.

Always check the property before rewriting an existing mortgage.

Follow the Land Records

The mortgage forms recommended do not permit the transfer of your mortgage to a new homeowner, nor do they permit the mortgagor to add any additional mortgages. As you might imagine, those limitations are not self-enforcing. There is no way to compel adherence to them other than by noticing the change in status and confronting the new owner or the original mortgagor.

Keeping abreast of changes may be much simpler than you think. Many local newspapers periodically list the community's real estate transactions. Look for the listings and glance at them whenever they appear.

If no listings are available, visit the town's real estate record room once or twice a year.

Keep in Touch

I recommend periodic personal contact with the mortgagor. Once a year will suffice, and a letter is almost as effective as a telephone call. If you have no reason to communicate, create an excuse.

"I just called to tell you how pleased I am with the prompt way you have been making your monthly payments."

"You probably don't realize it, but your payments have been arriving quite late. I have payments to make on the first day of the month myself, and, as much as I dislike being late, when your check arrives a week late, mine must, too. Please try to mail your checks on the thirtieth of each month."

Don't overdo it, but maintaining contact with your debtors reminds them that Big Brother is watching. An annual reminder that the name on their mortgage is a human being, not an impersonal corporation, increases the probability that your debtor will extend himself to cooperate.

Your Psychological Needs

The specific recommendations I have made are not necessarily the best for you. Only you know the time you have available, the personalities of your mortgagors, and the approach that best suits your own personality. Please, never hesitate to substitute your policies for those I recommend, providing your changes are merely one of degree. If your alterations in technique are radical, undercutting the very essence of the conservative approach so vital to successful mortgage investment, perhaps you had best change your media.

Nothing is more destructive of peace of mind than playing a role someone else has chosen for you that is totally unsuited to your emotional needs. This is particularly so with regard to investments. A nervous man, easily aggravated by rapidly shifting fortunes, should never invest in cyclical stocks that are perpetually bouncing to and fro. Nor should such a man follow his stock investments from day to day, eagerly scanning the stockmarket reports and noting each fluctuation. It will serve no purpose other than to make his life miserable. As experienced traders will attest, there is only one certainty on Wall Street — prices will fluctuate.

The adventurous soul, always seeking excitement, eager for the thrills of rapidly unfolding events, should invest in horse races, poker hands, or low-priced and high-flying speculative issues. Were he to purchase a stock portfolio of conservative public utilities, their uniformity and minor fluctuations would compel him to sell them in a very short while.

That same aggressive personality, eager for the excitement and agitation of continually changing circumstances and rapidly altering conditions, would suffer agonies managing a portfolio of formulized, conservative mortgages.

If your metabolism craves nervous excitement and adventure, pass this book on to someone else. To simple souls like myself, the moderate stirrings of finance and temperate venturesomeness of realty analysis that are the foundations of conservative mortgage investment are as daring a financial adventure as we are willing to undertake.

Swingers Need Not Apply

If you know, deep down, that you will chafe at the bit, that you will resist using our formulas, that your approach will be an aggressive, free-wheeling one, you have made a serious mistake. Mortgages cannot provide the excitement you crave. You will change the recommended patterns and lose your money just as surely as you would at the track or in Las Vegas, but not nearly as flamboyantly nor as quickly. It may take years.

Besides, there's no status in dropping a bundle in negligently chosen mortgages. People will perk up their ears when you tell them about your uranium mine or your visit to Las Vegas, but they will never stand still to hear your tale of foreclosures. It just ain't chic.

But if you are a moderate soul, if you find mastery of a new skill an exciting adventure, if your needs are satisfied by the quiet type of success that means security for your family rather than the quick buck and the nervous laugh, if your conception of gratification is attaining a working knowledge of one small sector of the world of finance and through that knowledge gaining increased stability, come on aboard. Trains leave regularly. The itinerary will not please everyone, but for those who will respect the rules, for those who will expend the effort, the trip will open a new world. Once completed, the satisfied traveler, armed with the experience of his first journey, will be able to move onto other tracks and out to other lands.

No, Virginia, Money Is Not Everything

Next stop? Real estate, perhaps. Whatever the choice, the lessons learned here will stand you in good stead. Appreciation of the benefit of total examination before commitment is the key to every investment field. Comprehension of the mechanics of the market place of money is a preliminary requirement of all successful investments. The people you met while mastering the mortgage field will open doors. The reputation you earned for keen analysis and conservative values will be your introduction.

Strange as it may sound, your most gratifying reward will not necessarily be the cash flow you generate or your expanding net worth.

Your most satisfying achievement may well be the quiet gratification that comes from taking on a challenge, meeting it head to head, and emerging victorious, armed with new skills, new knowledge, and a new sense of achievement. The quiet pride, the calm confidence, and the deep contentment are rewarding enough.

The money is a bonus.

20

Liquidating Your Portfolio

The Final Attribute ... A Ready Market ... Establishing Value
... The Going Rate ...Locating the Purchaser ... A Single
Package ... Money in Your Pocket ... Serenity ... Upward and
Onward

The Final Attribute

We have reviewed many advantages of the second mortgage as an
investment vehicle: the high rate of return, the conservative nature of
prudent choices, the ability to gain leverage through the use of other
people's funds, the relatively small amount of money necessary to
initiate your investment program, and the security that protects your
loan. All of these have been discussed in detail.

One final, joyous attribute of second mortgage investments has
merely been alluded to in passing. Liquidity: The ability to turn the
investments into cash, the advantage of being able to remove yourself
from your investment program whenever circumstances dictate.

Stock brokers urging investments in common stock of those major
corporations listed on the New York Stock Exchange proudly cite the
liquidity of the listed stocks as major considerations for their purchase. They unanimously affirm that the assurance of finding ready
buyers is an asset of considerable import.

Without the ability to liquidate, an investor can neither meet
serious emergencies nor enjoy the sweet taste of investment success
when his retirement years arrive.

For that reason, the purchase of stock in closely held corporations is generally not recommended. The purchase of some forms of real estate may face the investor with agonizing months of sales attempts, during which the price is often lowered to encourage prospective, but reluctant, purchasers.

A Ready Market

Your second mortgages will not stagnate nor will they compel you to painfully pursue reluctant purchasers.

Your second mortgages will find a ready market. Prospects will urge you to make your portfolio available to them.

If you will notice, I did not say second mortgages will not stagnate. The phrase was *your* second mortgages will not stagnate.

The difference between the average second mortgage and your second mortgage is the difference between and I.O.U. written during a clandestine poker party and a secured note signed at the desk of the Loan Officer of your neighborhood commerical bank.

The degree of liquidity to which I refer is characteristic only of those mortgages written in a form similar to that recommended, extended to mortgagors meeting our criteria, placed on properties conforming to our standards, and administered in the manner described. Mortgages of that type are investments. To the degree that they vary from our standards, other mortgages are calculated risks.

Mortgages of your quality are a rarity, an uncommon commodity. The higher risk mortgages, poorly phrased, improvidently placed, or informally administered, earn no more than your gem. They do run greater risks, however, and give rise to more aggravation.

Establishing Value

How do we determine the value of your mortgages?

Simple. Refer to the sample loan reduction schedule reprinted earlier in this book. If you have received seventeen monthly payments, merely run your finger down the column reading "Payment" until you reach "17." Pass along to the second column, reading "Amount Applied to Interest," and the third column, reading "Amount Applied to Principal," until you reach the final set of figures.

The heading of that fourth column will read "Balance of Loan." Whatever figure appears on the seventeenth line of the "Loan Balance" column will be the value of your mortgage.

Interest earned but not yet collected should be added, of course.

The Going Rate

Now that you have determined the value of your mortgage, will you be able to realize that much money upon the sale of your legal documents?

Yes, but.

Yes, you will, but only if your interest rate is that rate common to the community in which you will attempt to consummate the sale. If the investment community has established a 9 per cent pattern and your mortgage note calls for 7 per cent, you must anticipate selling your mortgage at a discount that would raise the rate to the established 9 per cent pattern.

This problem will not normally arise, particularly if you have followed my advice and sought the assistance of an attorney in your community. He will know the custom of the area and guide you accordingly.

Locating the Purchaser

Once again, having found the current value of your mortgage investment, will you be able to sell it for its full value?

Yes, but.

Yes, you will, but only if you have become familiar with other investors in your community and know to whom you should offer your pampered portfolio.

Obviously, unless you know where to turn, you will need help. Help generally costs money. But in this case, the cost will be relatively minor.

Mortgage brokers who generally charge 2, or sometimes as much as 3 per cent, to locate and process mortgage investment opportunities for prospective mortgagees, will be pleased to market your portfolio.

Certainly, preparing for the sale of an existing mortgage, the file of which already contains a credit report, an appraisal, an analysis of

Ability-to-Pay and your Safety Formula, requires infinitely less of a borker's time, effort, and expenditures.

As a matter of fact, the minimal cost, effort, and time might result in the broker's willingness to handle the sale of your investments at less than his normal fee.

In any event, the charge will generally be no more than three cents on a dollar.

If the mortgage brokers are not available, or if you prefer to do your own marketing, an advertisement in a local newspaper should solve the problem, and at a cost considerably less than the broker's fee for a substantial portfolio.

The advertisement should not be a modest one. Cite all the statistics that make your mortgages such conservative investment vehicles. The response will impress you. Many people will leap at the opportunity to benefit from your acumen and invest their funds in such a secure mortgage program.

A Single Package

I would not advise you to permit prospective purchasers to pick and choose within your portfolio. Your investments are not tomatoes for sale on an open-air pushcart. They are a single package, available as a package at one total price. Do not be stampeded by an early offer to buy a small portion of your package, or an adamant insistence upon a discount. Thank the scavengers for their interest, and show them to the door.

If more than one prospective purchaser combine to purchase your entire portfolio, consider such an offer as you would an offer from one prospect. A combination offers you the same benefits as an individual.

You may well find that the number of replies indicate an uncommonly eager atmosphere. Capitalize on it. Don't accept the first offer at par. Jot it down. Thank him. Tell him you will contact him within forty-eight hours. Then tell the next interested party that you already have an offer at 100 per cent of the face value. Would he be interested in raising his offer?

Particularly in a community where brokers dominate the second mortgage market, investors become conditioned to paying a few percentage points for their mortgage investments. You may find that your mortgages will bring $1.02 or $1.03 for each $1.00 of face value.

Money in Your Pocket

There are three stages within the history of a mortgage investment when the conservative approach we have been discussing means money in the investor's pocket. Literally.

The first occurs when an occasional mortgagor is unable to meet his monthly commitment. An investor who has followed the Safety Formula approach is assured of weathering the crisis. Either another investor will be willing to substitute his mortgage loan for yours, thus paying your mortgage balance directly to you in exchange for a release of your mortgage, you will be able to resort to a court of law in an action to foreclose your mortgage and recover the entire balance due.

The second stage at which the conservative approach literally means money in your pocket occurs when you approach a banker to negotiate a loan, offering your portfolio as collateral. The caution reflected in the quality of your mortgage investments will deeply impress him. He cannot help but respect a percentage of mortgage to appraised value superior to that of the community bank's mortgage departments. You will get your loan, and your leverage.

Money in your pocket.

The third stage is the final curtain. When you seek to liquidate your investments, prospective purchasers will react just as enthusiastically as the banker did.

If you have followed the pattern recommended in earlier chapters, the papers involved in each mortgage will be collected in one folder.

The credit report will be there for your purchaser's evaluation. In a moment or two he will know precisely why you consider the mortgagor such a fine risk. You will be able to dramatically illustrate his ability to pay, or his continuity of employment.

The appraisal will be available for his examination. Describe the conservative approach that you follow in settling upon the value of the property. Demonstrate the Safety Formula. Ask him to tell you what percentages of appraised value the banks are offering new mortgagors these days. That should clinch your sale right then and there.

But go further. Show him the mortgagor's record of monthly payments. If you have followed our Ability-to-Pay approach, the mortgagor will have the capacity to pay promptly. If you have followed our interview techniques and our techniques of encouraging timely payments, the mortgagor will have acquired the habit of paying promptly. His payment schedule will be a tribute to your investment skill — and the extraordinary value of your mortgage portfolio.

Once again, money in your pocket.

Serenity

It now becomes obvious that the techniques described in earlier chapters serve many purposes. They secure your investment. They provide leverage by encouraging bankers to lend you money for further investment. They assist you to liquidate your portfolio.

The techniques are not theoretical. They have all been born in the market place and been perfected in the commercial arena. They work.

Don't apologize for them. Don't question their basic wisdom. Apply them.

In discovering this area of second mortgage investment you have chanced upon an uncommon vehicle for supplemental income. You can invest in mortgages and still enjoy a good night's sleep. Not many investors can make that statement. Care to take on the aggravations of building an apartment house or picking a portfolio of accelerated growth stocks? How about buying some unimproved acreage on the outskirts of town or drilling for oil?

In these hectic days of continuing tension, when ulcers threaten to become our national symbol, how sweet it is to find an investment refuge far from the tranquilizers and sleeping pills.

Upward and Onward

But never confuse a conservative mortgage with warm milk and toast.

There is excitement in finance. There is a discernable pleasure in mastering the skills of the market place, becoming conversant with your local realty market and banking policies, and earning the reputation of a skilled and prudent investor.

You will mature rapidly in your new field, and develop skills you once envied in others. As a matter of fact, if you take my message to heart and apply its teachings, within the life of your initial second mortgage investment, you will become restless, having mastered this first rung on the economic ladder. You will know enough about real estate and banking, enough about administration and analysis, to move on to other things. All within the life of that initial mortgage investment.

When that day comes, and it surely will, sooner than you believe, resist the temptation to abandon second mortgages.

Your next step will inevitably involve more risks. Balance the odds by keeping a sizable portion of your funds in the secure hands of a mortgage deed and note.

If you dispose of your mortgage investments completely, you may rid yourself of the valuable lessons they teach, and the high standards they represent. That would be a very serious mistake.

Index